EDITED BY

GARY PAUL NABHAN

The
NATURE
of
DESERT
NATURE

THE UNIVERSITY OF
ARIZONA PRESS
TUCSON

The University of Arizona Press
www.uapress.arizona.edu

ISBN-13: 978-0-8165-4028-0 (paper)

Cover design by Leigh McDonald
Cover art: *Wild in the Plaza of Memory* mural [detail], by Leanne C. Miller, Ajo, Arizona.
Designed and typeset by Leigh McDonald in Arno Pro 11/15 and Cutright WF (display)

Ofelia Zepeda's essay on p. 51 originally appeared in *Interdisciplinary Studies in Literature and the Environment* 4, no. 1 (Spring 1997): 85–90. Francisco Cantú's essay on p. 105 originally appeared in *Territory* online magazine, no. 3 (2016). "A White Body Out in the Desert" on p. 116 is from *Eyes to See Otherwise / Ojos de otro mirar: Selected Poems*, by Homero Aridjis, edited by Betty Ferber and George McWhirther, New Directions, 2001.

Publication of this volume was made possible in part by the financial support of the Kellogg Foundation, Jim Hills, and the University of Arizona Southwest Center.

Library of Congress Cataloging-in-Publication Data
Names: Nabhan, Gary Paul, editor.
Title: The nature of desert nature / edited by Gary Paul Nabhan.
Other titles: Southwest Center series.
Description: Tucson : University of Arizona Press, 2020. | Series: The Southwest Center series
Identifiers: LCCN 2020011821 | ISBN 9780816540280 (paperback)
Subjects: LCSH: Deserts. | Desert ecology. | LCGFT: Essays.
Classification: LCC QH88 .E94 2020 | DDC 577.54—dc23
LC record available at https://lccn.loc.gov/2020011821

Printed in the United States of America
♾ This paper meets the requirements of ANSI/NISO Z39.48-1992 (Permanence of Paper).

CONTENTS

DESERTS SEEN FROM OTHER PLACES

DESERT AS ART / ECOLOGY NEXUS

ACKNOWLEDGMENTS

This multicultural collection of essays and art on desert life has been supported by subventions from James Hills and the W. K. Kellogg Endowment to the Southwest Center at the University of Arizona. It was inspired and fueled by the terrific team at the Desert Laboratory on Tumamoc Hill involved in art/ecology collaborations that speak more fully to our sense of place. In addition to the authors, artists, and staff at the University of Arizona Press, I am grateful to numerous friends and mentors who enriched or clarified my thinking and feeling about the nature of deserts: Delores Lewis, Amalia Astorga, Felipe Molina, Laura and José Kerman, Amadeo Rea, Eric Mellink, Julian Hayden, Raymond Turner, Ted Fleming, Byrd Baylor, Tony Burgess, Judith Bronstein, Rob Raguso, Alfonso Valiente Banuet, Humberto Suzán-Azpiri, Laura Monti, Jack Loeffler, Richard Rohr, Roy Johnson, Caroline Wilson, Roseanne Hanson, Lorraine Eiler, Alejandro Aguilar Zeleny, and Betty and Homero Aridjis.

THE NATURE OF DESERT NATURE

*A Deep History of Everything that Sticks, Stinks, Stings, Sings, Swings,
Springs, or Clings in Arid Landscapes*

GARY PAUL NABHAN

Being Splashed by Aridity

Our deepest knowledge of most places in which we have lived and loved—a landscape or the edge of a seascape—may well come to us in waves. Yet, what if our recognition of *desert nature* comes to us in dowsing splashes, hot flashes, or sharp-edged gashes?

Perhaps our recognition of what a *desert* is or can be does not simply come to us through some rational process of steadily accumulating knowledge over time. Instead, perhaps we learn what is memorable about deserts through a more imaginative process, one that comes in fits and starts, by solving riddles and reflecting on paradoxes, by abandoning dualisms and junking our prejudices.

Of course, there have been many prejudices—or at least, presumptions—about what a desert is and what it cannot possibly be.

The Comcáac (Seri), Yoemem (Yaqui), Tohono, Hia c-ed, and Akimel O'odham (Piman) people who first introduced me to desert living left me with a sense that a desert is an enchanted place. They may have imparted that sensibility to others as well, for when Spanish slave trader Nuño Beltrán de Guzmán encountered an elderly Yoeme shaman leading bow-carrying warriors to stop the Spanish in their tracks, he saw they were accompanied in their defense of their Sonoran Desert homeland by dogs, deer, birds, "and many other things" (Evers and Molina 1992; Hu-de Hart 1981). For them and many others, a desert is where hummingbirds, butterflies, bats, coyotes, deer, and flowers shimmer and sing in a resounding chorus from the first light of dawn through the rising of the moon (Evers and Molina 1987; Hill 1992).

And yet, over the arc of Western history, it seems that once a particular place is called a *desert*, we tend to ignore the enchantment and dwell in the dry facts, postponing the process of deeper, more exuberant, or reflective exploration. Sometimes, we fail to see the shimmer or hear the cacophonous chorus at sunrise. In fact, many men and women have stopped thinking about deserts once words like *deserted, desolate, sterile, abandoned, impoverished*, and *empty* first cross their minds.

When we dismiss the possibility of enchantment in all that deserts might be and mean, we do so at our own peril, or at the cost of not engaging with multiple wonders as we intensely experience many pleasures and certain pains.

So, I am here with good news: a fresher, *nondualistic* way of perceiving deserts has recently emerged in the natural sciences and in the arts that echoes and enhances an older way of imagining the desert found in the spiritual traditions of many ancient desert cultures. The shimmer is recognized, and the cacophonous chorus is heard once again.

I suppose that I was first desensitized by categorical dismissals of "low-productivity landscapes" while growing up in the Indiana Dunes, even though my childhood haunts in sandy habitats were *not* true deserts by any stretch of the imagination. Although I remember conversing with jays and sucking the juices from the sweet stems of wildflowers sprawling over the sandy hummocks, I never remember any adult speaking of this dunes landscape as an enchanted world.

What I do remember is how our visitors from other parts of the Midwest callously responded to *our* sand dunes while on short holidays away from their Corn Belt farms. They might gaze up at Mount Tom—the highest dune on our horizon—snap a photo of it with their Brownie cameras, then turn around and walk back to the car.

"You might say it's kind of purdy in its own peculiar way," I can recall—or at least paraphrase—one of our guests saying. "But all that wasted space—how can you grow anything in all that sand?"

"Nothing grows here?" I asked myself that day in the dunes. (I sometimes ask that same question when hearing newcomers react to the Sonoran Desert, too.) Sure, soy or hybrid corn might not last here on their own for long, but prickly pear cacti and whiptail lizards don't count? Grapevines sprawling over sandy hummocks do not matter? Neither do long-jawed orb weavers, Karner's blue butterflies, sundial lupines, or carnivorous sundews?

If a few hundred acres of dunes constitute empty space, then do the great American deserts—the Chihuahuan, Great Basin, Mohave, and Sonoran—collectively compose the *big empty*?

Perhaps the skeptics thought they had the desert pegged or, worse yet, surrounded and captured. But what if neither they (nor we) can ever capture all that a desert might be?

As architectural historian Reyner Banham (1982) once proposed, "In a landscape where nothing officially exists (otherwise it would not be *'desert'*), absolutely anything becomes thinkable, and may consequently happen."

So what if the desert is not empty, but full? Or what if it is simultaneously empty and full in a way that you have to tilt your head back and forth to see? What if you have to silence yourself not only to hear what the desert speaks, but to stay in conversation with this chimerical changeling?

And that, my friends, is what this book is about: *finding fresher ways to tilt our heads and silence our rants to experience a wider panoply of what deserts might be.*

The essays collected here are from artists, botanists, contemplatives, cultural historians, ecologists, field journalists, former border patrolmen, geographers, indigenous scientists, natural historians, oceanographers, philosophers, photographers, poets, river runners, singer-songwriters, and wanderers of many creeds, cultures, and countenances.

In their totality, these provocative and evocative essays reject dualistic ways of explaining the behavior of deserts. We might just need to abandon such false dichotomies about deserts, just as Einstein had to abandon the dualistic notion that light behaves *either* like particles *or* like waves to discover the essential paradox of illumination.

The authors featured here have had their senses opened and minds changed by repeated forays into desert places over many decades. Their stories are not so much about coming to firm conclusions regarding the nature of desert life. Instead, they may be about shedding our mistaken notions and "protective skins" as we become more open to knowing desert life in raw and previously unforeseen ways.

To be sure, I have stepped out into what I assumed to be an apparently monotonous, unproductive patch of arid landscape, only to have my own identity turned inside out by what I saw, heard, and smelled there.

This recently happened to me on the drought-prone coast of the Sonoran Desert between the Colorado River delta and Puerto Libertad, Sonora. It is nested in terrain that can go thirty-six months without measurable rainfall.

Once I listened, looked around, took a good whiff of the air there, my senses convinced me that I had been wrong headed about the paucity of life in that place.

At first, I saw nothing but squat, wind-beaten, drought-damaged, salt-stained shrubs with lots of barren space between them, as if the lack of water had forced the bushes from living closer to one another. None of the creosote, bursage, brittlebush, or saltbush were in flower; in fact, they seemed to be rather dormant, if not dead.

The horizon was dull edged and hazy from a recent sandstorm. Nevertheless, the sun beamed down on me with what seemed to be a preternatural force.

I stood there alone (I believed), silent enough to hear my own heart beating and the breeze brushing at my sleeves. I could not immediately figure out the patterns of the place—the relationships among weather, substrate, flora, fauna, and human influence.

A dust devil, or *chachipira*, suddenly swept by me and then disappeared into thin air, leaving bushes rustling and empty beer cans rolling around in eddies.

Then my eyes began to tear up in brightness, and I wiped them clean with a sweep of my shirtsleeve. Instantly, I was looking at this world as if I had come to another planet for the very first time.

The dull gray shrubs I had left for dead were actually in bud, their delicate tissues tenderly green. I began to see the cryptogamic crusts coating and protecting the soil between these bushes.

A tarantula sauntered by me, nonplussed by my presence. What (or who) does she eat in a place like this?

A silky-gowned phainopepla flew over, with a sprig of mistletoe in her mouth as she landed to roost in a mesquite tree and unpack her breakfast of berries. She dropped a few partially ingested seeds on my head and shoulders for good measure. I could feel what she had been eating.

A wake of turkey vultures circled high above me, patiently waiting to see how long it would take me to die. Just why, I wondered, are they so attracted to faintly fetid decomposing flesh?

What I had first dismissed as a haze-muddled horizon was one that actually had sharply contrasting features nested within it, as dark lava and pale granites interdigitated like hands folded together. A small black and white mountain range on the northern horizon appeared as though shaped by some goddess who loved sundaes made with Rocky Road ice cream.

The somewhat barren, jet-black lava flows at its summit spilled over the pale granite beneath them. Edging the paths of decomposed granite were antennae-like ocotillos and towering saguaros, as if they were part of a garden of freshly hewn sculpture, recently set out to dry.

Skirting the range on one side was an improbably large platoon of cardón cacti, most of them many armed and forty feet tall or more, with not a single nurse plant—a mesquite or ironwood tree—among them.

How could that be? I wondered, since I know that few cacti or stem succulents germinate and survive their first years out in the open. When and why did all their nurses and godmothers—*nodrizas* and *madrinas*—disappear from sight? Or were they never there at all?

Did the former inhabitants of this place have anything to do with the current scarcity of trees? For whom (and for how much) did they harvest them? Whom did they work for? To whom (or to what force) did they pray? Did they pray through song or through silence?

As I scratched my head and wondered how the giant cardón cactus arrived and settled here but nowhere else in view, I began to realize that I was in a landscape filled with unanswered questions and improbable paradoxes.

That is when I realized that the makings of a desert might never be fully known unless one goes underground. If true, the definition of a desert should be reframed to something like this: *a seemingly austere landscape in which there is always more than meets the eye.*

And so, I plunged underground, imaginatively speaking. Of course, there were myriad microbes cohabiting with plant roots deep beneath my feet, but just what do they do when the sand around them dries down? Do their hyphae or nodules dessicate or contract, or merely go dormant for a while? What would a termite or sand slug do when drought and heat penetrate past the soil surface? Do they go deeper, or die?

Of course, the desert extends into the sky as well, always carrying with it a palette of colors far different than those of tropical and temperate zones. There were feathery clusters of seeds flying over my head, destined for some secret landing strip nearby, and enough pollen to make me sneeze for weeks on end.

When I closed my eyes to sneeze, I noticed that I was not the only instrument in the orchestra. Cicadas were droning a metallic home not unlike that of Tibetan throat singers. Cactus wren, Gila woodpeckers, and Gilded flickers were offering raucous percussion. Yes, there are moments when the desert choir is *In a Silent Way* much as Miles Davis was. But many other mornings, they are more like "Los Mariachis" and "Ysabel's Table Dance," Charlie Mingus and his jazz band played his *Tijuana Moods*.

I was beginning to get a sense that I was not at all alone in some big empty. In fact, there was a dynamic coexistence of many lifeforms before me, with the particular mix found in any habitat patch due to the way different growth forms are favored or discouraged in different years by sun, sand, salt, volcanic substrates, drought, downpours, heat, and catastrophic freezes (Burgess 1995).

As my old desert rat friend Tony Burgess has reminded me over the years, "those lifeforms are in dynamic *disequilibrium* with one another. No single strategy for desert living is successful under all conditions."

I conceded that I had long been "wrong headed" when it comes to discerning what a desert comprises.

Such "belated" realizations now spilled over me like massive waves, tidal waves that surged up before I knew it and knocked me over.

Have your assumptions ever been sent tumbling "ass over tea kettle" in such a manner? Have you felt a new wave of realization surging up all around you, one that plasters you flat against the sand or the rocks?

When that happens, we must simply get up, brush ourselves off, and for a moment at least, recognize that we have somehow been humbled and changed in our relationship to the world. The world that may soon be known as Planet Desert.

When we dry off—and we dry out—we often forget that puzzling enchantment. Fortunately, another wave splashes down on us, and another. Soon the rhythm of the desert has taken over our sense of time and space.

Then and only then do we have a chance to sense fully what a desert is and is not, and what it can be in and of our own lives. That is why I had to nod in agreement when I first read what Egyptian American scientist Farouk El-Baz (1998) so clearly states: "Desert landscapes are the least understood among terrain types of the earth."

When I initially thought this assertion over, I rebelled a bit. Deserts may be something more than the least understood of all terrains. Deserts may also be *the* landscapes on this planet perceived, understood, and celebrated (or cursed) in the widest range of ways. How we regard deserts will vary greatly with our perceptions and professions, as well as our palpable life experiences.

Most Western-trained ecologists will use a language to describe deserts that is different from that used by an indigenous shaman on a vision quest; a contemplative from the Eastern Orthodox or Muslim faith; a landscape artist whose work lies outside galleries; or a poet who writes her poems on paper pressed from the fiber of desert wildflowers.

I recently recalled how I first gained insight into this chimerical quality of deserts while on the road with a bunch of desert ecologists led by that legendary Tony Burgess. Tony is not only a talented plant geographer but a great storyteller and field guide as well. Eight of us had the good fortune to accompany him on an excursion across all four North American deserts. That excursion was one of many he coordinated nearly forty years before our recent conversation.

Tony and I were among the only American-born participants on the excursion, which included distinguished desert scientists from the former Soviet Union, China, India, and Egypt. In ways most enlightening, but sometimes amusing or frustrating, each of our fellow travelers brought along a different mindset of what a desert might be, and how life within each landscape was structured.

At each field stop along our pilgrimage route—from the eastern edges of the Chihuahuan Desert in Texas through the Sonoran, Mohave, and Great

Basin Deserts—Tony would enlighten the foreign visitors on the species of plants and animals present at the site, as well as on its soils, climate, and environmental history.

The scientists were all delighted to see "in the flesh" many of the desert organisms they had read about over their illustrious careers. They recognized some species related to ones they knew back home. They were conversant with the landscape ecology of other deserts around the world. And so, the information flow was not just in one direction, from American ecologists to foreign visitors. They too had their own ideas about what we were seeing, hearing, smelling, and touching.

At one of our many roadside stops in the Chihuahuan Desert, Nina Nichaeva, from the Institute of Deserts in Russia, noted that we were witnessing a well-balanced desert *phytocenose*, where all the plants were sharing available resources and working "for the common good."

"Well, wait just a minute," said a Texas range ecologist whom Tony had invited to join us out at the site. "How does that explain that mesquite tree over there that looks like it is being killed by the prickly pear cactus around it that are competing with it for moisture?"

"Excuse me, please," the elegant elderly Chinese forester with us replied. "Look again." This desert forestry expert was also a master at combining various aromatic herbs into medicinal plant composites offered for use at Chinese *people's pharmacies*. "Both are still growing for now, and I believe that is because of the curative properties of the many herbs growing beneath their canopies. These appear to be potent herbs: *Ambrosia, Artemesia, Berberis, Datura, Solanum,* and such. Perhaps they are the glue that keeps this desert vegetation cohesive and healthy."

"My grandfather back in India would say that each has its own spiritual power," said the cinematographer, who was documenting the work of natural resource scientists through the lens of agricultural communications.

Our companion from Egypt, a petroleum chemist, was somewhat befuddled by all the Latin names of the plants and animals that Tony had been imparting to the group. He finally spoke up: "Do you mean to tell me that way out here in the desert, all of these plants have names of their own? All I wish to know is this: which of these plants can produce enough hydrocarbons to make biofuels after we run out of all of our fossil fuels in the desert?"

After that multivocal conversation, I could never again assume that the desert I was seeing was *not* a chimera, a sandcastle of many rooms, towers, and balconies standing high and dry above the desert floor.

The Ying/Yang of Nondualistic Desert Life

So what is the nature of life in the desert, its salient features, the classic structures, and characteristic behaviors an arid existence generates? Do we simply continue to stereotype deserts as "unproductive landscapes," or idealize them as sharply edged wilderness sanctuaries? Could they be both at the same time (Butterfield et al. 2010)? Are their openness, their austerity and elegance values that only contemplatives, philosophers, or artists assign to arid landscapes, or can those values factor into a broader definition of deserts for all of us?

Those very questions, my friends, may be older than Moses, for they are ones pondered by many souls over the millennia.

They are questions asked by many cultures dwelling in deserts, by their charismatic visionaries, by their marginalized outcasts, and by their self-exiled hermits who have settled in what more dominant cultures consider "open spaces" between "civilized" metro areas.

Yet, no matter how long the debate about the nature of desert life has proceeded, it seems that the essential questions remain ambiguously answered, and the debate remains largely unsettled.

In truth, the debate about the nature of desert nature today is in much the same state as the debate about the nature of light was among physicists a little more than a century ago.

The ongoing discussion about deserts, however, has generated and refined a certain set of questions that may be more pertinent to our own survival today more than ever before. *That is because of the degree to which global climate change is already forcing an ever-larger proportion of the world's human inhabitants to deal with ever more hot, dry, and sparsely vegetated landscapes.* These recently *desertified*, or biologically impoverished landscapes—which often lack the integrity and diversity found in ancient deserts—are becoming all too common on every one of the major continents.

That said, our initial responses to this set of questions may reveal more about our own dualistic psyches, political economies, modes of inquiry, and Western philosophical prejudices than it reveals about the physicality of arid landscapes in and of themselves. Deserts need not be seen as *either* empty or full, impoverished or rich, as danger zones or as sanctuaries, as fragile landscapes as opposed to resilient ones.

What if they could embody both conditions in each of those contrast sets, rather than one or the other? Could it be that neither response in the binary opposition of narrowly formulated answers gets to the ultimate question of what deserts can be?

To cut to the chase, what if we find that the ultimate reason to *dwell on* the nature of arid landscapes—and to *dwell in* those landscapes for a time—is so that we may be stunned, surprised, and disoriented, so much so that we may let our restrictive prejudices dry up, flake off, and drift away?

As postmodern philosophers have argued, what we refer to as *deserts* at this point in human history may be considered as much *cultural constructs* as anything else (Soule and Lease 1995; Gersdorf 2009).

These philosophers wish to deconstruct our notions of the desert, arguing that there is no such thing as a single objective reality of arid landscapes that cannot in some manner be contested. These illusions are less about the chimerical qualities of arid landscapes and more about our own mindsets.

Yet, as poet John Daniel (1994) has famously argued, let a sidewinder leave you with a venomous snakebite to deal with alone, and you might think twice about considering desert life nothing more than an intellectual construct.

Let me just slither and slide between these two rather dualistic views to explicitly state what may have already become obvious to most of you: an emerging view of the nature of desert nature has abandoned most knotty dualisms. Instead, we can liken a desert landscape to a prism, through which each observer from a different culture, discipline, or political ideology sees it in a different light. And yet, just as the prism is a palpable multidimensional entity—a concrete material with an existence independent of any intellectual attempts we may make to circumscribe it—so too do arid landscapes exist in a realm independent of our thoughts.

Yes, deserts *are* good to think about, but they are also delightful to viscerally experience as they swing us between hot and dry to foggy and cold, from quiet to violent, or from resilient to brittle conditions, whether we "wish" them to do so or not.

For me, at least, dealing with the desert in a nondualistic manner allows some creative tensions and complex dimensions to dramatically emerge and become delightfully apparent. These unanticipated tensions and dimensions have enriched my own life as a desert dweller and as a beginning student of anything that stings, sticks, stinks, springs, swings, or clings in arid landscapes. I try to take a "beginner's mind" with me whenever I venture into the desert alone.

Recently, some scholars of ecology, environmental history, and philosophy have undertaken collaborations in an attempt to produce "a richer understanding of nature than either one [of these opposing poles] can generate independently" (Eliot 2011). Some see this endeavor as a collaborative project toward "a philosophy of nature" writ large (Godfrey-Smith 2009), while others consider it to be part of what they call "deep history" (Shyrock, Smail, and Earle 2011).

That said, let us now descend into some of the desert's own deep histories, to understand how deserts distinguished themselves from other landscapes and biotic communities. Just as phenomenologist Gastón Bachelard (1957, 1964) offered us a psychoanalysis of fire and a poetics of space many decades ago, perhaps we need to undertake a "psychoanalysis of aridity" and a "poetics of desert habits and habitats" as they have been chanted across centuries of geological and cultural history.

Stepping into the Deep Muck of History Regarding Aridity

One of the most quixotic realizations I have ever gained about the nature of desert life came from a rather famous paleoecologist I met in person only once. At that meeting, I was at the beginning of my career as a field scientist when he was near the end of his illustrious one. His name was Daniel

Axelrod. Axelrod helped me fathom the far-reaching implications generated by a rather simple observation: the shaping of the iconic lifeforms that now dominate arid terrains and the emergence of the most emblematic species of the desert biota predate the formation of deserts themselves.

By the time I heard Dr. Axelrod speak about this principle, he was a wizened elder who did not need to defend his early scientific conclusions about the deep history of desert life. In fact, he conceded that many of the features, traits, and behaviors that he (and others) had used to identify, characterize, and "essentialize" *what desert life is about* did not initially evolve in full-formed deserts. They seem to have emerged in more tropical climes, in many plant families, and even in faunal phylogenies long before deserts themselves emerged as discrete entities. So is the tropics the true mother of the desert?

Perhaps, but not entirely. In his classic essay published in the *American Naturalist* in 1972, Axelrod reminded us that several kinds of "edaphically arid" sites have long occurred on unusual patches of rock or soil in or near tropical rain forests, subtropical thornscrub, and semiarid savannas. By examining plant fossils, he surmised that there have always been a few peculiarly dry habitats nestled into the moister matrix surrounding them, whether that matrix was truly tropical or not.

Of course, the plants and animals that reached these "arid islands in a tropical sea" had to adapt to highly seasonal rainfall followed by lengthy droughts. Many also had to adapt to *edaphic aridity*, that is, the poor moisture-holding capacity of their soils. The term *edaphic* has long been used to describe the physical (and largely abiotic, or lifeless) constraints placed on organisms by the substrate they grow within.

In Axelrod's mind, certain plants (for he largely ignored their microbial and faunal associates) finely adapted themselves to periodic drought, pervasive heat, and the limited capacities of certain soils. He hypothesized that rather early in floral evolution, some plants evolved morphological adaptations or biochemical processes to retain moisture and resist radiation damage during times of stress. Most of the kinds of plants that later flourished in deserts first caught wind in their evolutionary sails in what Axelrod called "dry edaphic sites in ancient terrains" that were essentially arid microniches scattered across an otherwise mesic milieu. In short, Axelrod contended that controlling factors of seasonally variable climates and poor soils had already been shaping the evolution of floras and their attendant faunas and microbes for thousands or millions of years before deserts differentiated themselves from other kinds of landscapes and vegetation.

At first, they may have lived in relative isolation on cliff faces or in lava flows, in rain shadows or in parched substrates derived from gypsum, limestone, or volcanic cinders well before they assembled themselves into desert vegetation associations. Only later did they assemble into more cohesive associations. Only then did the biotic communities that we now regard as being characteristic of desert landscapes gain much of a foothold on the earth's surface.

To grasp of the origins of the deserts of North America, then, we must first look southward for answers—in the Neotropics of Mesoamerica. But we must not forget other clues hidden in the dry forests of the Sierra Madre and the Rockies, along sandy coasts or open plains.

What strikes me as rather amusing about this urge to look elsewhere for desert origins is that *most notable ecologists and writers who focus on North American deserts had their personal origins elsewhere as well.* Most grew up in and knew tropical or temperate climes well before they began to explore the ecologically distinctive aspects of deserts themselves.

In other words, like the ancient flowering plants that Axelrod and others studied, most ecologists who came to work in deserts had come from wetter, cooler climes. The wet-to-dry trajectory of their journeys inevitably colored the way they responded to deserts. They saw an abundance of atmospheric humidity and soil moisture as the "normal" or "optimal" conditions for life as they had first known it. And so, the relative low humidity and soil moisture deficits in deserts struck them as abnormal or at least as unusual.

The Perils of Being Defined by What You Lack

It comes as no surprise, then, that some early explorers believed that drier landscapes "lacked" certain essential elements that were commonplace where they had spent their formative years. In the writings of many pioneering desert ecologists, agronomists, and poets, you catch some vague sense that they are describing a landscape that has some pathology or some inherent deficiency to it.

If unlimited rainfall is your only indicator that plants and people will be productive, healthy, and of value in a particular landscape, then overhauling that landscape (with water or technology) is the only cure for correcting its inherent shortcomings.

What an irony: Deserts may be the only landscapes in the world defined by most cultures in terms of *what they lack* rather than by the uniqueness of *what they have*. The oldest known cognate of the word *desert* comes from an ancient hieroglyph. It was likely pronounced "tesert." This term *tesert* refers to a place that had been "forsaken" or "left abandoned and emptied" (El-Baz 1988).

The Latin verb *deserere* ("to abandon," or "to vacate"), as well as related nouns and adjectives in Latin and in most Romance languages, were all derived from this disparaging root. More than any other measure, the singular notion that arid landscapes may lack something essential to life shaped most of what has been written in the Romance languages about the nature of desert nature.

Now, compare that sensibility with ones from people who have lived in deserts for thousands of years: Tohono O'odham or Desert Pima, and the Comcáac or coastal Seri—both indigenous cultures of the Sonoran Desert. In the Piman language of the Tohono O'odham, which they call O'odham *ha-nioki*, the term most akin to *desert* is *tohono*. It can best be translated as "a bright and shining place," that is, a place of reflectance and, perhaps, of human reflection. In the native language of the Comcáac, which they call *cmique iitom*, the term that most closely aligns with *aridity* or *desert* is *hamatj*. I loosely translate it as "(a place with) conditions dry enough to trigger thirst or dehydration." It is etymologically related to a verb, *caaxit*, which means "to cause thirst" (Moser and Marlett 2005).

To me, the sensibility of this term seems more like a reality check than a disparagement.

We can see from these lexicons and reveries the possibilities for deserts to be embraced as something other than depauperate, unproductive versions of tropical or temperate landscapes. Arid-adapted plants and animals have always had value beyond the desert's edge and will be increasingly important as parts of the planet become hotter and drier.

As for the desert itself, it is a place that can be refreshingly delicious, comforting, and nourishing as long as you find ways to stay hydrated and shaded. It is place where sound travels like nowhere else on earth. It is a place that can suddenly become luminous because of the peculiar optical qualities of its "wondrously glorious light." It is indeed a bright and shining place, not a dull, monotonous one.

The Paradox of Naming the Desert for an Oasis

Deserts and oases are like scratchboard etchings of each other, seeming polar opposites. Oddly, their respective "natures" are hitched at the hip in ways we seldom acknowledge.

I recently pondered this paradox while hiking through Nacapule Canyon, where a well-watered island of tropically influenced vegetation occurs near the Sonoran Desert's southern edges, on the coast of the Sea of Cortés (Felger, Carnahan, and Sánchez-Escalante 2017).

At first, I was dumbfounded and delighted to see tropical figs and native palms thriving in this hidden canyon, which is surrounded for miles by landscapes of tall columnar cacti and short but thorny legume trees. It seemed like an anomaly plopped down amid the Sonoran Desert, as if a wet tropical meteor had crashed down on a dry planet.

But in this case, the patch of tropics actually stuck and was stitched into the desert fabric. When I looked around me in every direction, I could see tropical influences in other plants there as well, from pineapple-like *Hechtias* to elephant-trunked *Burseras*. The acacias, agaves, limberbushes, seagrapes, and wild chiles I encountered in Nacapule had just as much standing in the wet tropical deciduous forest and the drier subtropical thornscrub as they did in the desert. They did not belong to a single "club" but were influential in all three communities.

We can now see such paradoxical juxtapositions in a new light. Landscape ecologists recently proposed that desert floras and faunas evolved and diversified from the first colonizers of mesic oases surrounded by drier terrain.

About the same time, I was astonished to learn that the Sonoran Desert— arguably the most uniquely diverse of all deserts in North America—was not named for its intensely arid and wild terrain but for a spring-fed wetlands surrounded by a scatter of houses and cornfields. Think for a moment about the irony of naming an entire desert expanse for a diminutive oasis in its midst.

In truth, the naming chain is a bit more complicated than the sound bite I just offered you.

The Sonoran Desert—where I have lived for more than half of my life— was named after a geopolitical region known as the province of Sonora before the war between the United States and Mexico split this bioregion in two between 1849 and 1851.

But an *informe* written in 1730 by Padre Cristobal de Cañas makes clear that the province was not named for its stunningly hyperarid *despoblados*, but for its artesian-fed cienegas, or wetlands, found within close reach of an ancient human settlement (Molina Molina 1979; Radding 1997):

> The most elderly indigenous people who remain alive tell me that the name *Sonora* comes from a marshy spring about a half a league from *Guépaca* [present-day Huepac, Sonora, Mexico. That is where] a large *ranchería* settlement [of the Opata culture] used to make their *jacal* houses out of river reeds and maize husks, which they call *sonot* in their indigenous [Uto-Aztecan] language. When the first Spanish heard their word, they pronounced it *Sonora*, and from then on, the whole province took this melodious and rather pleasing name.

Of course, we typically name an archipelago for the speck-like islands strung like rosary beads across a swath of sea, not for the sea itself.

According to linguistic anthropologist Jane Hill (2001), *sonot* may be one of the oldest and most widespread terms in the Uto-Aztecan language family. I have seen it variously translated as "spring-fed fields," "cornfields," "oasis," "place of irrigated corn cultivation," "*pueblo de milpas*," or "*ranchería de agricultura de temporal.*" The latter terms refer to a scattered settlement around rain-fed cornfields.

The first settlers of European and North African descent were probably obsessed with finding oases in the desert when they came north, up the coast from tropical Mexico, or west, from the temperate regions of the United States to the more arid reaches of western North America. Carrying a pejorative notion in their heads of what an expansive desert could be, they chose their native neighbor's place name for a particular spot that was most *un*desertlike and spread it out to cover the entire region. It was an oasis, an exception to aridity that not only proved the rule but offered a comforting image of an island of tranquility in a sea of conflagrations and cursed conditions (see Pfeffercorn, below).

Just what were those cursed conditions? In the writings of the Jesuit Ignaz Pfeffercorn about his early sojourn into the Sonoran Desert between 1794 and 1795, the padre begins his commentary on the "Natural State, Climate and Fertility of Sonora" by noting negatives. The "Good Father of Peppercorn" observes at that time "extensive plains where there is no running water," but then he quickly notes the oases where "scarcity is now and again relieved [only] . . . by a spring issuing from the earth or by a deep slough" (Treutlein 1989).

The German Jesuit then writes, "As a rule, not a drop of rain falls from the beginning of January to the end of June. . . . Consequently, the earth as well as the air is greatly parched by the sun's burning rays, augmented by the so-called *quemazones*, or conflagrations. . . . This season is very dangerous."

Drought, the burning sun and its unrelenting heat, the competition for access to potable water, questionably edible plants, and scarce game were certainly key constraints that could trigger conflicts among desert dwellers. Moreover, the fear of the unfamiliar overwhelmed many of the earliest Europeans who tried to settle in the desert. It appeared—at least by the architecture of plants and animals that dominated many of the most arid landscapes—*to be on the offense* against any human intrusion.

The Multifaceted Essence of Spinescence

If the desert were a ruthless ruler of a bellicose empire, we might offer the honorific title of Her Thorniness or His Horniness to this prickle-covered terrain. One of the first palpable impressions most of us gain from our encounter with a desert landscape is that it is armed to the hilt. It is armored with all matter of thorns, horns, spines, stinging trichomes, stickers, prickles, bristles, barbs, razor-sharp teeth, godawful glochids, and hooked hairs.

When Andrés Pérez de Ribas first saw the spinescence surrounding the pitahaya fruit of the organ pipe cactus in southern Sonora in 1644, he had this much to say: "The fruit grows from these thorny-ribbed branches and is, of itself, surrounded by a cover of thorns" (Pérez de Ribas 1968). Two decades later, another Spaniard, Miguel del Barco, noted, "When the blossoms dry and [the fertilized embryo] begins to swell, it is [so] covered with thorns that you can't see the fruit itself. As the fruits increase in size and are about to mature, the thorns become more widely spaced, and you can see through to the skin of the fruits, be they green, yellow or red, as when completely ripe" (del Barco 1980).

The desert might be saying to us "you might wish to be on guard." As my friend the Chicana poet Patricia Mora (1987) once reminded us,

> The desert is no lady.
> She screams at the spring sky,
> Dances with her skirts high,
> Kicks sand, flings tumbleweeds,
> Digs her nails into all flesh,
> Her unveiled lust fascinates the sun.

It is no genteel esquire, either. The desert's plants and animals appear as though they are ready to attack or hijack anyone who crosses their path.

Listen to their names: Horse-crippler cactus. Devil's claw. Spiny-tailed iguana. Prickly poppy. Desert spiny lizard. *Mala mujer.* Gila monster.

It is true: my forearms and shins have been riddled with scars, stabs, and tattoos from trying to break away from the clench, capture, and cuts inflicted on them by prickly pears, desert spoons, chuckwallas, wait-a-minute bushes, catclaw acacias, and pin-cushion cacti.

Despite all this armature—which seems so well suited for going on the offense—the first desert ecologists ask us to look again. They became convinced that this artillery was only for self-defense. Defense against browsers, grazers, and those who would dare try to penetrate the soft flesh of actively growing meristems, tender seedlings, delicate flower buds, ripened fruits, and such.

All this spinescence offers sanctuary against the hooves, horns, antlers, leathery tongues, sharp teeth, and claws of Wild Things that love nothing more than to stomp and chomp on otherwise vulnerable beings of the vegetal and reptilian worlds.

That explanation of the essence of spinescence fared well in over a century of naturalists' commentaries about the nature of desert life. Then, both anatomists and physiologists of desert biota discovered that only half of the picture regarding armature had been elucidated. The thorns, horns, and spines surrounding barrel cacti, saguaros, chollas, ocotillos, and even horny toads perform other functions, such as reducing heat loads and water loss from organisms, as well as increasing water availability to some.

In some rather stunning cases, a heavy armature of spines actually attracts mammals to cacti rather than repelling them.

When physiologist Park Nobel began to look at what the presence of spines did to the growth and survival of barrel and cholla cacti, he found that their influences are a mixed bag. For barrel cacti, three-quarters of their stem surfaces are shaded by hooklike spines, while the spines of the teddy bear cholla offer a third of the surface of the radiation-sensitive stems some protective shade, thereby "cooling their jets."

Nonetheless, here is the catch: the spines reduce both damaging radiation, especially to hypersensitive actively growing meristematic tissues, and photosynthetically active radiation. The latter is essential for plant growth and reproduction. In fact, the spines buffer the stems for damaging light, as well as extreme heat and cold, so that these plants survive catastrophic freezes and heat spells. Surviving during those times of high stress was undoubtedly a tradeoff worth investing in, even if it meant slower growth rates of the stems during optimal weather.

Nobel has guessed that these protective factors alone might allow for these cacti to extend their ranges into both colder and warmer regions than they would have been able to do if they were spineless. In fact, some cacti succumb to sunburn and ultimately die if their spines are clipped, singed, or scraped off their skins. Nevertheless, Nobel does not deny the role that spines play in defending cacti from herbivores. His sense is that barrel cacti have denser spines over their fast-growing apical regions to protect these sensitive areas from both herbivory and temperature extremes, rather than one or the other.

The either/or argument that spines reduce either biotic stresses from browsers *or* abiotic stresses from temperature extremes flew out the window. That dualism was put to rest by Park Nobel's ingenious experiments on desert plants.

About the same time that Nobel was pioneering such work on cacti, my friend Wade Sherbrooke (1990) was doing somewhat comparable work on horned lizards (*Phrynosoma*), the reptiles we fondly call horny toads in the Sonoran and Chihuahuan Deserts. He was well aware that the horns surrounding the lizard's crown and the teethlike protrusions on the ridges of its back and along the edges of its belly have often deterred predators from killing and swallowing horny toads. Sherbrooke noticed that these protrusions and the microscopic *integumental* drainage ways between and beneath them greatly aid the lizards in harvesting rainwater. The rainwater collects on their backs and rains toward their mouths so that they can drink it immediately after brief desert rains.

In essence, beneath and between all those horns, teeth, and scales are interscalal channels that drain most of the water falling on the horny toad's flattened back down toward its mouth. By lowering its head, then rapidly opening and closing its jaws, the horny toad is able to conduct most of the rainwater harvested off its body into its mouth. North American horny toads are not the only lizards to pull off this trick. The thorny devils (*Moloch*) of Australia and the endangered sunwatchers (*Phrynocephalus*) of Asia Minor also use their armature to guide harvested rainwater down toward their mouths.

More recently, another evolutionary irony was discovered in the deserts of Utah: "defensive" cactus spines can attract white-throated packrats to consume the very plants that are most heavily armed by such spines. Some of these packrats have long specialized on feeding on cholla cactus stems, having developed counter-adaptations to the defenses that the plants have evolved to protect themselves.

The packrats not only tolerate the oxalates in cactus stems, which are indigestible to other mammals, but have also found ways to clip off the spines on the stems with their teeth to target the most highly nutritious stems available in their home range. Curiously, the packrats seem disinterested in stems that have been artificially despined by humans, since they typically have lower nutrient content if left to grow "exposed" for a while before the packrats encounter them.

Utah ecologists Kevin Kohl, Aaron Miller, and Denise Dearing (2014) surmise that the packrats are using the spinescence of cholla cactus joints as a proximate cue that attracts them to stems with higher protein and lower fiber content than despined stems.

When considering all the roles that spines, thorns, horns, and teeth may play in the lives of barrel cacti, teddy bear cholla, horny toads, and white-throated packrats, we are left with a wonderful set of paradoxes. Conventional dualistic thinking can hardly deal with such paradoxes.

The richness of these desert adaptations *emerges from the multiple roles* that these arid-adapted structures can play in the survival, vitality, and vigorous growth of both plants and animals. Binary either/or thinking simply cannot take us far in our attempts to more deeply understand the essence of desert life.

Choose Your Poison: Fragrance or Venom?

When we get out of hiding completely within our heads and come to our senses about what a desert may be, why does each of us perceive it so individualistically yet so distinctly?

To be sure, some people may be appalled by a desert's odiferousness, while others are enthralled by its enticing fragrances. Some who have tasted its most putrefied fruits can never wipe their palettes clean, nor rid their memories of such putridity, while others have tasted something so delectable that it has left them weak in the knees.

All these sensory pleasures and horrors may be present in the very same desert landscape. Our memories of them are prone to gravitate toward one extreme or another, rather than simultaneously holding both experiences together at the same time, in some dynamic balance or creative tension.

An O'odham child once told me that *the desert smells like rain*, a rather quixotic juxtaposition, don't you think? Chemical ecologists tell me that the fragrance of desert soils after the rain smell like *geosmin* or *petrichors*, and the creosote bushes smell like *phenolic resins* (Sequín 2018; Palermo 2013). I know that they are technically correct—but it seems they forgot the magic that O'odham child of the desert fully experienced.

Let's take the example of a desert plant whose leaves taste too sharp to encourage consumption by many browsers, grazers, or chefs of haute cuisine. And yet, the flavor of its foliage is found to be quite desirable and deeply pleasurable by others, so much so that it demands premium prices.

The plants in question are the desert oreganos, variously named *Lippia palmeri*, *Lippia graveolens*, or *Lippia berlandieri*, depending what desert flora you are consulting. Their leaves exude two aromatic oils—thymol and carvacrol—that are the same phenols found in thyme, Greek oregano, beebalm, and other culinary herbs. But where I have picked their most pungent leaves was on the crest of a coastal range of the Sonoran Desert. There, the plant roots seldom receive more than four inches of rain per year. As drought drags on, they exude more of the thymol and carvacrol oils to coat their leaves as an antitranspirant to control water loss, and they produce smaller leaves for the same purpose. They also produce other oils, such as geraniol—the nonphenolic compound with a roselike smell in geraniums and beebalms—which hardly have much effect on their capacity to tolerate more drought.

To be clear, drought is not their only challenge. Browsers cannot be choosers during hot dry times, so the oregano bushes need enough thymols and carvacrols to repel herbivory, whether by bighorn sheep, mule deer, or other mammals of the desert. If the oregano plant is successful in surviving drought, high heat, and browsers, it becomes resplendent with fragrance and all-a-glisten with the sheen of aromatic oils. Miraculously, the foliage of these stress-tolerating shrubs is just perfect for those of us seeking a *desert terroir*—the divinely concentrated fragrances and flavors that make arid land cuisines so memorable (Nabhan 2012).

As in the case of teddy bear cholla, the defense strategy of desert oregano is not exclusively as a repellent against browsers or predators but also as a retardant against high heat and prolonged drought. But the texture, taste, and aroma produced by oregano's desert-adapted leaves are remarkably rich in potent chemicals: a sublime gastronomic experience to many (but not all) who wish to experience a desert cuisine built around the most potent plant and animal foods of arid landscapes.

In fact, desert plants are remarkably rich in potent chemicals: atropines, atrozines, bereberines, capsaicins, cucubitacins, l-hyocyanes, lophophane, mescalines, nicotines, peyotlines, protopines, pyridines, quinones, retrosines, sanguinarines, scopalomines, solanines, tropanes, and such. Desert insects and reptiles offer us a chemical arsenal of apotoxins or mellitins, wasp kinins, hornet kinins, and a wide array of neurotoxins, with a few alarm pheromones thrown in.

Few desert plant toxins and venoms blow no good. Scientists have already isolated byetta from the venom of Gila monsters, which may serve as an effective drug against type 2 diabetes, an affliction now common among Sonoran Desert dwellers. Other scientists are screening desert snake and lizard venoms to identify compounds novel to current pharmaceuticals that may "tune" the immune systems of humans and livestock species, upscaling immune responses to infectious diseases and cancer, while down-regulating the immune response during autoimmunity (Munawar et al. 2018).

Thus, the chasm begins to widen between what first awakened us to the desert's sensory panoply and what still lies just out of reach, unseen, untasted, or unheard.

Sometimes, we meet only what we seek and filter everything else out. Yet, in more fortunate times, these evasive "spirits of the desert" break in on our workaday lives, disrupting our staid conclusions and filling us with awe.

Silence and Sanctity Among the Sonorous and Raucous

One midsummer night on a mountain ridge overlooking the Sea of Cortés, two Comcáac (Seri Indian) elders left me alone at the mouth of a cave, to be silent, to fast, to listen, and to dream my way through a rite of passage.

I became just one more individual among many tens of thousands throughout history initiated into the sacred silence of a desert night.

During that dark night of my soul and into the *madrugada*, nectar-feeding bats flew between my arms and legs, honeybees covered my neck and shoulders, mule deer and javelinas graced the slopes below me, and turkey vultures circled over my dazzled head. But I heard no words, other than a Seri song I was gifted in my dreams against the measured beat of bat wings.

Over the course of many centuries, pilgrims, ascetics, hermits, and monks of countless cultures have sought out the silence and sanctity of desert contemplative traditions. One such tradition of quiet transformation is that which the Greeks have called *heyschia* (Burton-Christie 1993). One might argue that this tradition was never physically nor metaphorically dependent on dwelling in an arid landscape per se. Its expressions reached their zenith, however, in the Wadi al-Natrun region of Egypt known as the Desert of the Sceti, from whence our term *ascetic* emerged. In a broader sense, deserts seemed particularly conducive places for practicing this contemplative tradition, in the sense that attentiveness to silence, aridity, scarcity, poverty, and humility could often be more easily activated than in large cities or agricultural valleys.

Another time, I crawled hundreds of feet into a lava tube on the volcanic shield of the Sierra el Pinacate, just a dozen or so miles south of the U.S.-Mexico border. I kept my headlamp on until the last pang of fear of bats, scorpions, and snakes left my feeble mind. When no such phantoms appeared before me, I extinguished the head lamp and simply listened.

No sounds from the desert floor or sky just a few yards above me intruded on the lava tube. I kept my mouth shut and my mind as still as it would be. Any thought that sprang up was allowed to pass back out of my consciousness as quickly as it came in.

I was doing a centering prayer where there was so much darkness that I could never see the center. Sheer silence washed over me; it was a silence so pure that it seemed that nothing of the human world intervened to disrupt it. I sat ecstatic for minutes, grateful for having arrived in an aural wilderness.

After a while, I finally noticed a kind of sound that had been with me all along. It was the sound of my own heartbeat thumping, or being thumped, like a big bass drum. It was *felt* more than it was *heard*. It felt loud even though it might not have actually been audible.

The pumping of my own heart was the only sound that I could feel/hear for minutes more.

I knew that I was alive, alive in a fresh manner that the most arid of all places had gifted me. I was alive in a darkness and silence so undiluted that I could recognize only my own heartbeat within them.

I was fully alive in that silence.

Of course, others may regard the desert as raucous, with its ear-splitting sounds traveling and echoing far distances. I once met an O'odham boy at a school in Santa Rosa, Arizona, who considered the desert in which he lived to be extremely noisy (Nabhan 1995): "Those birds—they wake me up. The woodpeckers get on our roof and make so much noise." They seemed to be sharpening their beaks on the metal turrets placed on the roof, where air vents let heat and gaseous air out of bathrooms. They made a *rattta-tat-tat* sound, like a snare drum or machine gun.

The clatter was made by many birds—some, like flickers, wrens, and woodpeckers, I have already mentioned, but other voices chime in as well: Chihuahuan ravens, Gambel's quail, poorwills, white-winged doves, mourning doves, curve-billed thrashers, mockingbirds, and roadrunners all contribute to the syncopated rhythms. And let me not forget the guest appearances from other vocalists like cicadas, crickets, bumblebees, honeybees, and Sonoran and spadefoot toads.

Yes, the boy's desert seemed noisy. Mine was peaceful and quiet. Did we actually co-inhabit the same desert? Or were we living in altogether different worlds?

My tentative answer is that our worlds were very different, but not necessarily because our minds had intentionally or even unconsciously "constructed" alternative universes (Nabhan 1995; Gersdorf 2009). We were seeing and hearing the desert differently because of a kind of parallax that skewed viewsheds and soundscapes. And too, each species of desert rat, bat, bird, and reptile no doubt absorbs that soundscape in an altogether different manner.

Parallax, a term most often used in optical sciences and creative photography, denotes a positional difference between two views regarding an object in sight of each stance. This positional difference, however slight, between what the "viewfinder" sees and what the "film" records through the lens creates a tangible discrepancy between the two images. The O'odham boy and I were not seeing or hearing the world in the same way because of a kind of *cultural parallax* between us (Nabhan 1995).

Our hearing and seeing of Sonoran Desert landscapes not that many miles from each other had become differentiated by the degree to which we actively, sensuously participated in the dynamics of particular microhabitats. We lived along different stretches of some sensory gradient between barely inhabited and culturally diffused spaces, which then shaped the aural and visual images as well as the words we used to describe these places.

When I was in the lava tube and he was in a bathroom with a wind vent above, neither of us was sensing or thinking that we were in "the Sonoran Desert" writ large. We were each in touch with a microhabitat surrounded by aridity but different from it. Each of those imaginary habitats was habitable space, with real or phantom lives giving it some immediacy and intimacy. No doubt our personal histories lodged in our memories shaped those spaces as well. To paraphrase Heraclitus, "No man ever steps *into the same desert twice,* and two men can never find the same desert to step into."

It is likely that the boy and I cannot ever dip our feet into the same flow and splash of aridity in exactly the same way. In this sense, the abstract concept of *desert,* or even the more particular concept of Sonoran Desert, has little to do with how we live our lives in relation to how our neighbors live theirs. We share the gift of silence in the desert, but not the same meaning of the words describing it.

You Don't Miss Your Water till Your Well Runs Dry

When I was barely twenty-one, I went out to the desert isles of the Galapagos archipelago on a steamer, which ran out of potable water within four days of our departure from Ecuador's arid coast. We had no more water for showers, flushing toilets, or drinking at leisure.

That is how I first palpably learned about the anxious human obsession with scarcity and competition.

Coming from better-watered climes in the temperate or tropical forests, those newly arrived in arid terrains might unsurprisingly become obsessed with competing for water (Powell 1878; Weaver and Clements 1938). As Butterfield et al. (2010) suggested, early ecologists considered the ecological processes shaping plant communities in arid climes as "driven by abiotic controls [such as low rainfall and high rates of evaporation], with biotic interactions playing an insignificant role." And yet, a few of the more keenly observant European-born observers of the Sonoran Desert saw no inherent struggle or competition for water among the plants or animals there.

When Miguel del Barco (1980) concerned himself with whether water was a potential limiting factor in the deserts of Baja California, he gave his attention to the cardón cacti growing around the Misión San Xavier, in the southern reaches of that arid peninsula:

> This tree, although full of moisture, is found only on dry lands, on level and sloped ground alike, provided that there is no moisture nearby, for this it shuns. . . . Whence then does it draw that moisture and the sap with which it is replete?
>
> [They came] not from the rains, since these are very scant in California, and therefore, where there is no permanent spring and one must rely on rainwater alone, nothing can be sown or planted. . . . The cardón, however, even though years may pass without rain, shows no sign of distress: it perseveres serenely, with the same fresh green color and the same abundant sap, as ever.

Few early scientist-explorers saw a need to advance the notion that drought and water scarcity—as well as occasional catastrophic floods—had much of a *direct* role in shaping Sonoran Desert vegetation or their landscapes as a whole. It was not until the 1878 *Report on the Lands of the Arid Region of the United States* that explorer John Wesley Powell advanced such an obvious hypothesis.

Powell's argument was straight and to the point: there was simply not enough available water in the arid West—particular in the deserts of the Southwest—to support high-density populations of wildlife, livestock, or settlers compared with the densities already found in the more mesic eastern reaches of the United States. Powell assumed that unless his brand of rational planning allowed settlers to deal with the challenges of water scarcity, competition for water and conflict over it would be inevitable. As Kirsch (2002) has suggested, there is a dark Darwinist sense of tooth-and-claw competition in Powell's assumptions about the nature of the arid West.

Ever the number cruncher, Powell projected from his observations in the arid and semiarid landscapes of the West that only 1–3 percent of the territory between the 100th meridian and the coastal mountain ranges along the Pacific could support the consumptive lifestyles of the European Americans addicted to notions of westward expansion and manifest destiny. He doubted that they could achieve any substantive agricultural development, because of the paucity of potable water and the already voracious competition for it. Whether or not he was certain that competition for water took place among desert plants and animals, Powell was convinced that water scarcity would pit one human culture against another in the Great American Desert.

We have two views of how water scarcity may shape desert life. The first is that plants, humans, and other creatures can space and pace themselves to avoid competition and overconsumption of available water. The other view assumes that an inexorable thirst will force humans or other biota to compete with one another until the very last drop is swallowed.

Are these opposite sides of the same coin or views of the desert seen with blinkers on that limit any other possible scenarios?

Desert Vegetation as Anarchy or Cohesive Community?

One of the most hotly debated issues in the science of desert ecology, which emerged soon after Powell's report, was the repeated consideration of the nature of community in arid lands.

Community was a term being bandied about in both the ecological and social sciences in the late 1800s. Sociologists as well as environmental scientists were trying to figure out how different kinds of communities are differentially shaped by forces such as competition and cooperation. In a sense, this discussion harks back to a larger debate in the environmental and social sciences triggered by Darwin's theory of natural selection; here, I attempt to bring that debate to bear fruit on dry ground.

Different readers of Darwin, just like diverse observers of the Sonoran Desert, have come to widely different conclusions about the relative roles of competition and cooperation in shaping natural communities. Ecologist Douglas Boucher (1985) suggested, "While Darwin devoted a good deal of time to studying mutualisms, . . . there is no doubt that his fundamental contribution was that adaptation and speciation can be explained by competition."

Evolutionary ecologist Judith Bronstein (2011) agrees that there was such a bias in early Darwinian thought: "Darwin's influence has often been interpreted as deflecting attention away from beneficial phenomena in nature," as he usually focused rather sharply on the selective pressures emerging from competition.

Curiously, in at least one passage in *On the Origin of Species* Darwin (1869) offers an exception to this rule. He asserted that competition between and among plant species was likely not much of a factor in shaping the vegetation of extreme environments, such as warm deserts and cold tundra or taiga environments: "When we reach the Arctic regions, or snow-capped summits, or absolute deserts, the struggle for life is almost exclusively with the elements."

What a sweeping conclusion. In essence, Darwin was arguing that *abiotic* (climatic and geological) stresses shaped the structure of desert, taiga, and tundra life far more than biotic factors, such as competition, predation, or even cooperation between different lifeforms. While Charles Darwin and his son Francis shared a keen interest in what we now term the coevolution of plants and their insect visitors, the elder Darwin appears mute on the topic of whether such mutualisms significantly shaped entire biotic communities in deserts or other biomes he had visited in the world.

Nonetheless, while Darwin was still alive, another set of naturalists, natural philosophers, and biologists began to build a general theory of how mutual aid among species came to shape various plant communities and drive the diversification of life on earth.

The historically favored phrase *mutual aid* does not exactly mean the same as what *mutualism* means to scientists today, nor does it encompass the one-way benefits of their more recent term, *facilitation*. But in 1873, before the range of facilitative interactions among plants and animals was fully charted out, Pierre van Beneden coined the term *mutualism* to more narrowly refer to relationships where *one or more species* receive repeated and reciprocal benefits from another.

To place *mutualism* in the more specific historical context of the then-emerging field of ecology, the term was coined just a year after the discovery of the yucca–yucca moth relationship, a *symbiosis* that ecologists later recognized as the first known mutualism between a plant and an obligate pollinator (Pellmyr 2003).

By the end of the nineteenth century, many ecological relationships were being investigated as potential mutualisms or symbioses, and those discoveries generated discussion well beyond botanical gardens and zoos. They excited a Russian contemporary of Darwin's, Prince Pyotr Alexeyevich Kropotkin, who soon suggested that such mutual aid had far more effect than competition on the evolution and structure of both natural and human communities.

As an anarchist and socialist, Kropotkin ([1908] 1985) clearly drew parallels between the mutualisms between species and collaborative processes in human societies. He emphasized such ecological and social mutualisms as means to counter the political influences of social Darwinists, such as Francis Galton (Darwin's cousin) and Herbert Spencer:

> In the practice of mutual aid, which we can trace to the earliest beginnings of evolution, we thus find the positive and undoubted origin of our ethical conceptions; and we can affirm that in the ethical progress of man [as in nature], mutual support—not mutual struggle—has had the leading part.... It was an evolutionary emphasis on cooperation instead of competition in the Darwinian sense that makes for the success of species. (Kropotkin [1908] 1985, 300)

What is of interest here is that Darwin's and Kroptkin's comments foreshadow a larger and more lasting debate about the factors that most pervasively shape the adaptive interaction among individual plant species and, more broadly, the very nature of natural communities, especially those in deserts.

For decades, ecologists have battled over the degree to which desert plants and the way they aggregate with animals and microbes into identifiable assemblages are predominantly shaped by the physical stresses of drought and heat; by competition among species for moisture, nutrients, light, and space; or by facilitation involving soil microbes and invertebrates in ways that benefit dominant plants. In short, the very nature of cohesive desert communities was being contested by these discordant constructs and viewpoints. Ironically, it was an anarchist (Kropotkin) who put forth a view of cohesive vegetation communities being shaped by mutual aid more than by competition for scarce resources.

In the early twentieth century, ecologists such as Shreve and Gleason took another, so-called *individualistic* approach, suggesting that communities (if they existed at all) were loose assemblages shaped more by random *stochastic*, or catastrophic, events, disturbances, and competition than by facilitation and mutualism. To the extent that our views of natural communities mirror our views of whether there is an intrinsic coherence, goodness, and integrity in human communities (Worster 1994), these long-standing debates are ultimately about the essence of life itself.

Let us trace how this debate played itself out in one particular theater in the Sonoran Desert—the Carnegie Desert Laboratory on Tumamoc Hill, where an influential group of desert ecologists and artists assembled on the edge of downtown Tucson, Arizona.

A Desert Laboratory to Incubate and Test Ideas

By the late 1890s, there began to emerge a protracted interest in the ecology of North American deserts, mostly from well-educated Easterners and Northern Europeans who had taken short sojourns into the desert from more temperate climes (McGinnies 1981). Their expeditions were sponsored by educational, research, and land-management institutions anticipating dramatic shifts in the demography and economy of human communities in response to westward expansion. Their "colonial" explorers endeavored to determine which resources could be exploited immediately, and which should be conserved for later use (or no economic use at all).

At the same time, they stimulated the formation of a place-based community of desert botanists, ecologists, writers, and artists that has remained cohesive to this day (Wilder and O'Meara 2015). Scientific historians have argued that the nascent science of ecology was dramatically shaped by the dialogue between these early desert botanists and other ecological thinkers of their era (Kingsland 2005; Slack 2006).

I personally experienced the continuity and cohesion of this community of ecologically minded desert dwellers the first couple times I climbed to the summit of Pinacate Peak in northwestern Sonora. I was accompanied by ecologist Ray Turner, environmental historian Bill Broyles, nature artist Paul Mirocha on one trip, and Tohono O'odham leaders and park rangers on another. Each time we reached the summit, we performed a ritual that had been enacted many times over the previous century. Together, we ceremoniously stood on our heads like Pinacate beetles, just as William Hornaday, Jeff Milton, Godfrey Sykes, and Daniel MacDougal had done on their expedition nearly a century before. Nevertheless, despite the palpable collegiality shared by field scientists and cultural observers of Sonoran Desert life, they did not necessarily view the desert in exactly the same light, whether they stood on their heads together or not.

Some, such as the Norwegian explorer Carl Lumholtz, did not at all believe that drought and competition for water had much of a *direct* role in shaping Sonoran Desert vegetation. Lumholtz (1912) did concede, however, that wide spacing between plants was likely due to their need to capture moisture through their extensive root system over a large area, a notion that implies competition:

> Contrary to the popular conception of deserts, the one in question has a vegetation wonderfully adapted to its environment. During the year I spent there, I never saw any plant, bush, or tree suffering from want of rain, in spite of the fact that winter passed without its customary showers. Nothing appears scorched from the sun, for desert plants are slow to dry up as well as slow to grow. Next to the healthy though sometimes somber color of the vegetation and the scarcity of trees, that which strikes the observer the most when first traveling in the desert region is the isolation of each bush or plant. It is as if they were growing in a nursery. This arrangement is made necessary because the plants need large spaces from which to gather the scanty moisture, sending their roots out horizontally all around.

About the time that Lumholtz made these observations in the Sonoran Desert, the Carnegie Institution of Washington, D.C., began to staff its Desert Laboratory on Tumamoc Hill to undertake longer-term studies to more definitively answer such questions (Wilder 1967; McGinnies 1981; Wilder and O'Meara 2015). Although formally founded in 1903, the Desert Laboratory staff, facilities, and instrumentation were not fully fleshed out until 1906.

This remarkable scientist initiative staged in the middle of the desert soon attracted visits from the who's who in the natural sciences at that time, including William Hornaday of the New York Zoological Park, the most famous wildlife writer of his era, and Frederic E. Clements, the "first philosopher of ecology" (Tobey 1981). Clements and his wife, Edith, eventually spent parts of eight years (1913–1925) at the Desert Laboratory, ironically without ever publishing a single major paper or book dedicated to the topic of desert ecology. Like Brewster Higley, songwriter of "Home on the Range," it seems that the two Clementses "stood there amazed, by a glory greater than ours," for they were dumbfounded by how little the Sonoran Desert behaved according to Frederic's theories!

Clements's first visit to the Desert Laboratory preceded that of Forrest Shreve, whom he soon employed there. But not long after Shreve became a Desert Lab scientist, he became skeptical of Clements's vacuous theories and a thorn in the side of Clements's empire building (Bowers 1988).

That said, Clements's periodic presence at the Desert Laboratory is significant to the debate about competition and cooperation in arid landscapes. Influenced strongly by social Darwinism, Clements had emerged as the North American leader in the study of schematic classifications of all kinds of vegetation. He rigidly applied the analogy of plant communities as [super] organisms to identify, categorize, and treat types and stages of vegetation as discrete cohesive entities that remained "intact" through space and time.

A contemporary of Clements, the light-hearted ecologist Frank Egler (1951), once suggested that Clements was "driven by some demon to set up a meticulously orderly system of nature, as neatly organized and arrayed as the components of Dante's *Inferno*." While Christopher Eliot (2011) has recently argued that Clements was not as dogmatic as his critics later made him out to be, Clements clearly was not a proponent of Kropotkin's notion of relationships based on mutual aid among plant species. In fact, he gave only passing attention to mutualisms over the course of his forty-year career (Bronstein 2015).

Most histories of ecology assert that Clements's true nemesis was H. A. Gleason, not Forrest Shreve. As early as 1926, Gleason stridently challenged these assumptions as he meticulously documented the "individualistic" nature of plant distributions in North America (Gleason 1926, 1936). And yet, it is clear that many histories of ecology tend to ignore that Gleason's concerns were anticipated and initially raised in print by Forrest Shreve. In fact, Shreve took constant issue with any of Clements's presumptions about desert vegetation that appeared to come more from the truisms of social Darwinism than from observable patterns in the vegetation found on the Desert Laboratory's grounds (Bowers 1988). Such scathing critiques of Clements's notions—voiced in conversations on the Hill and printed in a journal edited by Shreve—may be among the reasons that Clements never published a single one of his own meditations on the nature of desert nature.

What Gleason and Shreve objected to were the hard and fast conclusions by Clements that the vegetation of deserts—and of prairies, forests, and wetlands as well—were cohesive associations with sharp edges, comprised of highly competitive species, a few of which prevailed through space and time. Their own observations and quantitative measurements favored the more individualistic nature of plant distributions along gradients that shifted with each landscape and geological period.

There is something endearing about the way Shreve humbly positioned himself as a field observer who nonchalantly reported what patterns he discerned, rather than acting like a strident ideologue. Here is a classic set of observations by Shreve (1964) about an apparent aggregation of desert plants that Clements might have concluded to be the formation of tightly structured desert communities:

> The colonies of seedling trees, small shrubs, grasses, and vines to be found under and around the larger trees or oldest shrubs grow denser toward the central and southern part of Sonora, and include many species not found in the open. As the subordinate colonies increase in density, they also grow in extent and spread beyond the shade of the tree. On the … Sonoran plains … the stand of large perennials become denser than it is in the north or west of there, at the same time that the subordinate colonies spread more widely. As a result, it is common thing for several colonies to coalesce and, with a group of fostering trees, to form a sharply defined motte, or island, of vegetation. Broad expanses of bare or sparsely covered ground separate the mottes. It is obvious that many conditions are concerned in making the establishment of new individuals easier in the mottes or around their edges than in intervening open areas.

Note how Shreve carefully avoids using terms such as *ecological succession* or *biotic communities* in this excerpt. And yet, despite both Gleason and Shreve's skepticism about Clements's categorical pronouncements, they continued to conditionally use the term *plant communities* over the rest of their careers.

Later in his career, Gleason (1936) tried to show that he and Shreve were pragmatists: "We must admit that a *stand* of vegetation is a concrete entity." Postmodernism had not yet infected ecologists' brains.

As for Shreve, he stuck to his guns in being aversive to abstractions. Although he accepted W. B. McDougal's 1918 article on "symbiotic phenomena" in his role as editor of *Plant World*, Shreve's own writings never used terms such as *facilitation, symbiosis,* or *mutualism*. Even when describing the rather tight relationships between desert nurse plants and other species found in the shade of their canopies, Shreve (1951) avoided phrases like *nurse plant guilds* by merely noting that "fostering trees" harbored under their canopies where "subordinate colonies of grasses, herbs, vines, cacti, and subshrubs [formed] denser vegetative mottes or islands."

Shreve (1951) later summarized his view on the relative importance of negative or positive biotic interactions with one short declaratory sentence: "The greatest 'struggle' of plants has not been with one another, but with the [physical] environment."

Ultimately, desert ecologists rejected the superorganism-like coherence of plant communities that Clements and his disciples had promoted. Perhaps just as influential was the fact that by the end of World War II, most Americans had simply moved on from their fleeting interest in "socialism" and, in some cases, from social Darwinism as well. As politics swing, so does ecological theory.

Ecology De- and Reconstructing Itself After World War II

Decades after Shreve and Clements passed on, Fritz Went, the elder statesman of physiological ecology, stirred up the desert dust once more. In a rather peculiar essay published in the prestigious *Proceedings of the National Academy of Sciences* in 1973, Went took up the issue of competition in deserts where Shreve had left off. Specifically, Went doubted that competition among plants in water-scarce deserts could be used as some supporting example of social Darwinism. He was skeptical that desert plants competed for any resources in ways as dramatic as the competition witnessed among animals as they struggled "with tooth and claw" against one another:

> Competition is a word of various meanings. In biology, it originally was introduced to account for the low survival rate of the potential offspring of all creatures. . . . With Darwin's evolution[ary] theory, competition took on additional meaning in relation to survival of the fittest. Competition was not anymore a struggle between equals, but a mechanism to award superiority. Competition became a contest, and considerations of combat, struggle, territorial exclusion, and even war entered in the wake of Darwin's ideas. As [earlier proposed] . . . competition is "a consideration of the means by which plants oust each other from habitats." But, it is hard to conceive of any mechanisms by which stationary plants can combat each other to result in an ousting. (Went 1973)

Went was already an internationally acclaimed botanist, plant physiologist, and pathologist when he became the director of the Desert Research Institute in Reno, Nevada, at the age of sixty-two. By coming into the North American deserts rather late in his career, he would perhaps bring insights into the nature of desert life unlike those of many other scientists of his era. Went had indeed witnessed true competition for light and space among trees in tropical rain forests. But after his decades of observing plant communities in moist temperate and tropical climes, he was unconvinced that desert plants ever truly "competed" against their neighbors for much at all. In fact, he concluded from several observations in Death Valley that competition— or biotic interactions in general—had no significant effect in shaping either the density or reproductive success of desert plants!

The timing of Went's sweeping conclusion was ill-fated. On the heels of his controversial paper in 1973, a new breed of evolutionary ecologists had begun working in deserts with altogether different tools, quantitative techniques, and hypotheses. Just a year after Went's publication in the *Proceedings*, Heithaus (1974) provided the first conclusive data that mutualistic relationships between plants and their pollinators had a profound effect on community structure. At the same time, other ecologists' long-term studies began to reveal clues that competition and cooperation among desert species were tangibly evident and profoundly influential on community structure (Brown and Davidson 1977; Waser and Real 1979; Heske, Brown, and Mistry 1994; Ward 2012).

The paradigm had quickly shifted. Everything was up for grabs again. While most of the new documentation of competition in deserts involved small mammals, several naturalists elegantly demonstrated that competition among desert plant species as well. The plants may not have been "jousting" or "ousting" their neighbors as Went wishes to see, but when competitors were packed too closely together, their growth, survival, and mating success diminished (Fowler 1986; Friedman 1971; Goldberg and Novoplansky 1997).

Let's just consider one of the most revealing field studies on how competition among plants intensifies or relaxes under varying desert conditions. Ecologist Deborah Goldberg and her team worked on the very same ground around Tumamoc Hill's Desert Lab where Shreve and Clements had battled it out. Goldberg's team revealed that the stiffest competition among annual desert wildflowers occurred *not when soil moisture or nutrients were unusually scarce* but during periods of availability of these resources for growth (Goldberg and Novoplansky 1997). Neither competition nor cooperation could exclusively explain everything about desert living. In fact, they could be two sides of the same coin that "flipped" when conditions changed.

Gradually, the most patient desert ecologists began to discern the subtle patterns of just when, where, and how competition, facilitation, and mutualism shaped desert plants and animal distributions along gradients (Holmgren, Scheffner, and Huston 1977; Bertness and Calloway 1994; Maestre et al. 2009; Butterfield et al. 2010; Gremer et al. 2013).

It seemed that no one any longer doubted that both competition and the facilitation of positive interactions were abundantly evident in most kinds of desert communities; in fact, they were hitched at the hip. As Milena Holmgren and colleagues (1977) suggested, there is often a dynamic interplay of cooperation and competition coursing through desert plant communities. As the lives of desert trees, cacti, and understory vines intertwined before her eyes, Holmgren offered this nondualistic perspective on their dance upon dry ground: *"[The] positive and negative effects of [nurse] plant canopies always occur simultaneously."*

In essence, recent teams of ecologists have offered us a synthetic view of desert lives that most desert ecologists may be able to live with for a while: Under the extreme conditions, plants may benefit from other plants' presence as a means to reduce the impacts of the stresses they shoulder, even more than they antagonistically compete with one another. But when stresses are reduced or absent, competition among desert organisms may flare up and become pervasive.

The pendulum swings across the stretches of desert.

Sorting Out Mutualisms from One-Way Facilitation

Why might it have taken desert scientists so long to agree on just how and when competition or cooperation occurs between desert plants in ways that profoundly shape the structure of their associations with one another, with the fauna and microbiota? Did they lack the tools or the vision to do this earlier?

In my own field studies with Mexican and American ecologists working as a seamless team, we have found abundant examples of facilitation, competition, and true mutualism in the same desert plant guild (Nabhan and Carr 1994). There are "one-way" facultative benefits that a nurse tree may provide to one or more "protégé" species (such as night-blooming cacti) that grow under its protective canopy (Suzan-Azpiri, Nabhan, and Patten 1994; Withgott 2000). There are symbiotic relations between the senita cactus and a pollinating moth whose eggs and larvae develop entirely within the flesh of the cactus (Fleming and Holland 1998). There is also competition between nurse plant and cactus severe enough for the cactus to kill its life-long nurse (McAuliffe 1984). Such varying interactions among desert biota led Butterfield et al. (2010) to make another nondualistic assertion about the nature of desert nature: desert plant community dynamics are under "the dual control of climate and biotic interactions."

To be sure, the notion of truly mutualistic interactions occur in desert communities—human or otherwise—is not novel. But for some reason, until rather recently, it was deemed a rarely expressed or exceptional phenomenon among desert plants and animals. Indeed, as late as the 1960s, George Williams (1966) asserted that "really good examples of mutualism are relatively rare" anywhere in the world, but especially in deserts. Even the great ecologist Robert May (1976) categorically dismissed them as inconspicuous features in most if not all ecosystems.

And so, the simple insight that mutualistic relationships are pervasive enough to significantly influence the very structure of desert biotic communities is a relatively recent one. That is so ironic, given the fact that the very discovery of the first obligate mutualism—among yucca flowers and yucca moths—occurred in the semiarid reaches of western North America in the mid-nineteenth century (Pellmyr 2003)!

It took naturalists a while to realize that the yucca flower–moth mutualism was not a one-of-a-kind outlier. Within the twentieth century, ecologists have discovered mutualistic relationships also among desert figs and fig wasps, agaves and nectar-feeding bats, and senita cacti with senita moths (Marazzi et al. 2015; Fleming and Holland 1998; and Holland and Fleming 2002.)

In the way that Marazzi and colleagues (2015) have regarded these various mutualisms, the presence of symbioses among plants and invertebrates in "the Sonoran Desert is well-documented and [scientists are] certain of its iconic interactions."

On a broader scale, ecologists Stone and Roberts (1991) have concluded from one survey that 19 to 50 percent of all interactions in various plant communities can be considered mutualistic. More specifically, pollination ecologist Jeff Ollerton (2006) has estimated that nearly nine out of ten flowering plant species in the world have mutualistic relationships with pollen-vectoring animal species, and such a high ratio seems to hold true in many desert landscapes.

There are agnostics on this issue. Dodds (1997) argued for a more conservative estimate that a sixth or less of all interspecies interactions are mutualistic. But Dodd's estimate hardly takes into account any interactions with desert plants or animals involving the microbiome! We tend to see only as far as our noses, but we seldom let our noses dig very deep underground.

Presently, the most underexplored locations of mutualistic relationships in deserts now appear to be in "the hidden half of nature," such as the nitrogen-fixing bacteria and fungi in the soils of arid landscapes or in animals' guts (Montgomery and Bilké 2016). As we delve into those dimensions of interactions among desert biota, arid land ecologists are likely to document hundreds more species in the Sonoran region who are engaged in true mutualisms. That revelation will radically shape what we imagine a desert landscape may be (Lynch 2008).

In a global survey of the soil microbiome beneath our feet, Fierer et al. (2012) found that desert microbial communities were clearly distinct from "nondesert" communities, no matter what metric was used. But how? The hot desert communities they studied had more microbial diversity than cold deserts. The microbiome in hotter deserts harbored lower abundances of genes associated with nutrient cycling and antibiotic resistance than did forests, grasslands, or tundra communities.

But here's the kicker: when compared with the underworld of forests, grasslands, or tundras, desert soils nurtured microbes with higher abundances of genes associated with osmoregulation and seasonal dormancy. In other words, desert mycorrhizae and other arid-adapted microbes have evolved myriad means of coping with environmental stresses. Clearly, some of these means can benefit their plant hosts and the animals that live in their root zones, trunks, canopies, or fruits.

Good science—like good art and good prayer—often humbles us and makes us wonder how little we actually know. It seems that we are barely seeing "through the glass darkly" all the dimensions of desert nature, and how it affects human nature. Through fits and starts, little waves and giant tsunamis, we have been stumbling upon a more expansive, integrative, and nondualistic view of desert life.

Embracing the Paradoxes of a Chimerical Desert

Over the last century, many physicists have embraced the view that light has a dual nature, simultaneously behaving like both particles and waves. We typically glimpse only one of these behaviors, depending on the experiment through which light is subjected. Most of us can admit that both waves and particles may be simplified models of reality, but we may still have difficulty giving equal weight to each in terms of how light exists. We may then concede that the physics of light may be such a complicated phenomenon that no single model from our own sensory experience can fully explain its nature.

It may also be true that biotic communities are much like loose assemblages of particles as well as waves splashing within the streams of life that meander across space and time. They are shaped by seemingly random physical processes. These processes generate physical and chemical stresses that either cull out or favor different species over others. And yet, they often move like eddies in a stream, forming highly cohesive, interactive biotic communities shaped by facilitation, interspecific communication, and mutualistic relationships just as much as they are by competition for scarce resources.

In noting the phenomenon of interspecific communication, I am not merely referring to songbirds of various species alerting one another to the presence of a predator. I am also referring to the growing body of (still-controversial!) evidence of how plants communicate with one another through their mycorhizzal connections, leaf chemistry, and distinctive floral scents (Raguso and Kessler 2017; Gagliano, Ryan, and Vieira 2020).

It may not be too much of a stretch to affirm that the desert may be "enchanted"—that is, filled with floral and faunal incantations—that our sophisticated scientific tools are only beginning to record. And yet I have known sensitive mimosa plants, desert lizards, tortoises, hummingbirds, dogs, and shamans who behave as though they have been sensing these many voices, vibrations, volatiles, and voltages all along.

We may someday have more precise tools to help us recognize how communications within and among these "chaotic assemblages of individual particles" and "eddies of intense ecological interactions" function. Nondualistic thinking can allow us to comprehend how these two facets of nature's order may be occurring simultaneously, but perhaps on different scales. In any case, both facets of organization appear to be co-located and embedded in the same structures of the living landscapes of Arid America.

Let us all humbly recognize that we inevitably construct and idealize our views of the Sonoran Desert every time we venture out into this world. We inevitably do this because of subtle and often subconscious influences on our thinking from politics, religion, art, architecture, and philosophy, not just from the tentative conclusions of so-called *objective* science. Perhaps the only sustaining benefit of participating in the exploratory processes of field science is that we humbly learn that our own tentative conclusions may be woefully inadequate in their explanatory power over the long haul. They are likely to be revised, amplified, or altogether junked by future scientists, philosophers, or theologians, who will look with fresh eyes, insights, tools, and ideas at the very same phenomena that have baffled us.

In the following invited essays (and two poems!), some of my dearest colleagues celebrate the many ways in which the human mind and heart have responded to arid landscapes. I have intentionally invited plant ecologists, animal ecologists, poets, singer-songwriters, environmental historians, aural recorders of soundscapes, contemplatives, border scholars, landscape artists, marine biologists, desert explorers, photographers, and natural history educators to consider what contemplating deserts might reveal. I want to "shake us up," to force us to lose our sure footing, so that we will be splashed with and swim through the desert's stream of energy in an altogether refreshing manner.

I encourage you to see, smell, hear, taste, and touch the desert as if you have been gifted with new eyes, noses, ears, mouths, and hands. And when you recover your wits and relocate your place in the enchanted desert, perhaps you enter into a fresh and exuberant relationship with everything that sticks, stinks, stings, sings, swings, springs, or clings in arid landscapes.

References

Axelrod, Daniel I. 1972. "Edaphic Aridity as a Factor in Angiosperm Evolution." *American Naturalist* 106 (949): 311–20.

Bachelard, Gastón. 1957. *The Poetics of Space.* Translated by Maria Jols. Paris: University Press of France.

Bachelard, Gastón. 1964. *The Psychoanalysis of Fire.* Translated by Alan C. M. Ross. Boston: Beacon Press.

Banham, Reyner. 1982. *Scenes in America Deserta.* Salt Lake City, UT: Gibbs M. Smith.

Bertness, Mark, and Ragan M. Calloway. 1994. "Positive Interactions in Communities." *Trends in Ecology and Evolution* 9:191–93.

Boucher, Douglas H. 1985. "The Idea of Mutualism, Past and Future." In *The Biology of Mutualism*, edited by Douglas H. Boucher, 1–28. New York: Oxford University Press.

Bowers, Janice Emily. 1988. *A Sense of Place: The Life and Work of Forrest Shreve.* Tucson: University of Arizona Press.

Bronstein, Judith L. 1995. "The Plant-Pollinator Landscape." In *Mosaic Landscapes and Ecological Processes,* edited by Lennart Hansson, Lenore Fahrig, and Gray Merriam, 256–88. Dordrecht: Springer-Verlag.

Bronstein, Judith L. 2015. "The Study of Mutualism." In *Mutualism,* edited by Judith L. Bronstein, 3–19. New York: Oxford University Press.

Brown, James H., and Diane W. Davidson. 1977. "Competition Between Seed-Eating Rodents and Ants in Desert Ecosystems." *Science* 196:880–82.

Burgess, Tony L. 1995. "Desert Grassland, Mixed Shrub Savanna, Shrub Steppe, or Semidesert Scrub? The Dilemma of Coexisting Growth Forms." In *The Desert Grassland,* edited by M. McLaren and T. R. Van Devender, 31–67. Tucson: University of Arizona Press.

Burton-Christie, Douglas. 1993. *The Word in the Desert: Scripture and the Quest for Holiness in Early Christian Monasticism.* New York: Oxford University Press.

Butterfield, Bradley J., Julio L. Betancourt, Raymond L. Turner, and John M. Briggs. 2010. "Facilitation Drives 65 Years of Vegetation Change in the Sonoran Desert." *Ecology* 91 (4): 1132–39.

Daniel, John. 1994. *The Trail Home.* New York: Pantheon Books.

Darwin, Charles. 1869. *On the Origin of Species by Means of Natural Selection.* New York: Appleton.

del Barco, Miguel. 1980. *The Natural History of Baja California.* Translated and edited by Froylan Tiscareño. Los Angeles, CA: Dawson's Book Shop.

Dodds, W. K. 1997. "Interspecific Interactions: Constructing a General Neutral Model for Interaction Type." *Oikos* 78:377–83.

Egler, Frank E. 1951. "A Commentary on American Ecology, Based on Textbooks of 1947–1949." *Ecology* 32:677–78.

El-Baz, Farouk. 1988. "Origin and Evolution of the Desert." *Interdisciplinary Science Reviews* 13 (4): 331–47.

Eliot, Christopher. 2011. "The Legend of Order and Chaos: Communities and Early Community Ecology." In *Philosophy of Ecology,* vol. 11 of *Handbook of the Philosophy of Science,* edited by Kevin deLaplante, Bryson Brown, and Kent A. Peacock, 49–107. Amsterdam: Elsevier.

Evers, Larry, and Felipe S. Molina. 1987. *Yaqui Deer Songs, Maso Bwikam: A Native American Poetry.* Tucson: University of Arizona Press.

Evers, Larry, and Felipe S. Molina. 1992. "The Holy Dividing Line: Inscription and Resistance in Yaqui Culture." *Journal of the Southwest* 34 (1): 3–46.

Felger, Richard S., Susan Davis Carnahan, and José Jesús Sánchez-Escalante. 2017. *Oasis at the Desert Edge: Flora of Cañón Nacapule, Sonora, Mexico.* Proceedings of Desert Laboratory, Contribution 1. Tucson: University of Arizona Desert Laboratory.

Fierer, Noah, Jonathan W. Leff, Byron J. Adams, Uffe N. Nielsen, and Scott Thomas Bates. 2012. "Cross-Biome Metagenomic Analyses of Soil Microbial Communities and Their Functional Attributes." *Proceedings of the National Academy of Sciences* 109:21390–95.

Fitzpatrick, Ginny, Goggy Davidowitz, and Judith L. Bronstein. 2015. "An Herbivore's Thermal Tolerance Is Higher Than That of Ant Defenders in a Desert Protection Mutualism." *Sociobiology* 60 (3): 252–88.

Fleming, Ted H., and J. Nathaniel Holland. 1998. "The Evolution of Obligate Pollination Mutualism: Senita Cactus and Senita Moth." *Oecologia* 114:368–74.

Flores, Joel, and Enrique Jurado. 2003. "Are Nurse-Protégé Interactions More Common Among Plants from Arid Environments?" *Journal of Vegetation Science*, April 9, 2003. https://doi.org/10.1111/j.1654-1103.2003.tb02225.x.

Fowler, Norma. 1986. "The Role of Competition in Plant Communities in Arid and Semi-arid Zones." *Annual Review of Ecology and Systematics* 17:89–110.

Friedman, Jacob. 1971. "The Effect of Competition by Adult *Zygophyllum dumosum* Boiss. on Seedlings of *Artemisia herba-alba* Asso in the Negev Desert of Israel." *Journal of Ecology* 59:775–82.

Gagliano, Monica, John C. Ryan, and Patrícia Vieira, eds. 2020. *The Mind of Plants.* Whiteriver Junction, VT: Chelsea Green.

Gersdorf, Katrin. 2009. *The Poetics and Politics of the Desert: Landscape and the Construction of America.* New York: Rodopi.

Gleason, H. A. 1926. "The Individualistic Concept of the Plant Association." *Bulletin of the Torrey Botanical Club* 53 (1): 7–26.

Gleason, H. A. 1936. "Is the Synusia an Association?" *Ecology* 17:444–51.

Godfrey-Smith, Peter. 2009. *Theory and Reality: An Introduction to the Philosophy of Science.* Chicago: University of Chicago Press.

Goldberg, Deborah E., and Ariel Novoplansky. 1997. "On the Relative Importance of Competition in Unproductive Environments." *Journal of Ecology* 85:409–18.

Gremer, Jennifer R., Sarah Kimball, Katie K. Keck, Travis L. Huxman, Amy L. Engert, and D. Lawrence Venable. 2013. "Water-Use Efficiency and Relative Growth Rate Mediate Competitive Interactions in Sonoran Desert Winter Annual Plants." *American Journal of Botany* 100 (10): 2009.

Heithaus, E. R. 1974. "The Role of Plant-Pollinator Interactions in Determining Community Structure." *Annals of the Missouri Botanical Garden* 61:675–91.

Heske, Edward J., James H. Brown, and Shahroukh Mistry. 1994. "Long-Term Experimental Study of a Chihuahuan Desert Rodent Community: 13 Years of Competition." *Ecology* 75:438–45.

Hill, Jane H. 1992. "The Flower World of Old Uto-Aztecan." *Journal of Anthropological Research* 48 (2): 117–44.

Hill, Jane H. 2001. "Proto-Uto-Aztecan: A Community of Cultivators in Central Mexico?" *American Anthropologist* 103:913–34.

Holland, J. Nathaniel, and Theodore H. Fleming. 2002. "Co-pollinators and Specialization in the Pollinating Seed-Consumer Mutualism Between Senita Cacti and Senita Moths." *Oecologia* 133 (4): 534–40.

Holmgren, Milena, Marten Scheffner, and Michael A. Huston. 1977. "The Interplay of Facilitation and Competition in Plant Communities." *Ecology* 78 (7): 1966–75.

Hu-de Hart, Evelyn. 1981. *Missionaries, Miners, and Indians: Spanish Contact with the Yaqui Nation of Northwestern New Spain, 1533–1820.* Tucson: University of Arizona Press.

Jimenez, Rocio, Maria P. Ikonomopoulou, J. Alejandro Lopez, and John J. Miles. 2018. "Immune Drug Discovery from Venoms." *Toxicon* 141:18–24.

Kingsland, Sharon E. 2005. *The Evolution of American Ecology, 1890–2000.* Baltimore, MD: Johns Hopkins University Press.

Kirsh, Scott. 2002. "John Wesley Powell and the Mapping of the Colorado Plateau, 1869–1879: Survey Science, Geographical Solutions, and the Economy of Environmental Values." *Annals of the Association of American Geographers* 92 (3): 548–72.

Kohl, Kevin D., Aaron W. Miller, and M. Denise Dearing. 2014. "Evolutionary Irony: Evidence that 'Defensive' Plant Spines Act as a Proximate Cue to Attract a Mammalian Herbivore." *Oikos* 124 (7): 1–19.

Kropotkin, Pyotr A. (1908) 1985. *Mutual Aid: A Factor in Evolution.* Boston: Extended Horizon Books.

Lumholtz, Carl. 1912. *New Trails in Mexico: An Account of One Year's Exploration in North-Western Sonora, Mexico, and South-Western Arizona, 1909-10.* New York: Scribner and Sons.

Lynch, Tom. 2008. *Xerophilia.* Lubbock: Texas Tech University Press.

Maestre, Fernando T., Ragan M. Calloway, Fernando Valladares, and Christopher Lortie. 2009. "Refining the Stress-Gradient Hypothesis for Competition and Facilitation in Plant Communities." *Journal of Ecology* 97 (2): 199–205.

Marazzi, Brigitte, Judith L. Bronstein, Pacific M. Sommers, Blanca R. Lopez, Eriquena Bustamante Ortega, Alberto Búrquez, Rodrigo A. Medellin, Clare Aslan, and Kim Franklin. 2015. "Plant Biotic Interactions in the Sonoran Desert." *Journal of the Southwest* 7 (2–3): 457–502.

May, Robert M. 1976. "Simple Mathematical Models with Very Complicated Dynamics." *Nature* 26:459–67.

McDougal, W. B. 1918. "The Classification of Symbiotic Phenomena." *Plant World* 21:250–56.

McGinnies, William. 1981. *Discovering the Desert.* Tucson: University of Arizona Press.

Molina Molina, Flavio. 1979. *Estado de la Provincia de Sonora por Padre Cristobal de Canas.* Hermosillo, Sonora: Diócesis de Hermosillo.

Montgomery, David R., and Anne Biklé. 2016. *The Hidden Half of Nature: The Microbial Roots of Life and Health.* New York: Norton.

Mora, Patricia. 1987. "Unrefined: The Desert Is No Lady." In *The Desert Is No Lady: Southwestern Landscapes in Women's Writing and Art,* edited by Vera Norwood and Janice Monk, ii. New Haven, CT: Yale University Press.

Moser, Mary Beck, and Stephen Marlett. 2005. *Comcáac quih Yaza quih Hant Ihíip hac: Seri Spanish–English Dictionary.* Hermosillo: Universidad de Sonora/Plaza y Valdés.

Munawar, A., S. A. Ali, A. Akrem, and C. Betzel. 2018. "Snake Venom Peptides: Tools of Biodiscovery." *Toxins* 10 (11): 474. https://doi.org/10.3390/toxins10110474.

Nabhan, Gary Paul. 1982. *The Desert Smells Like Rain.* Tucson: University of Arizona Press.

Nabhan, Gary Paul. 1995. "Cultural Parallax: The Wilderness Concept in Crisis." In *Reinventing Nature? Responses to Postmodern Deconstruction,* edited by Michael L. Soule and Gary Lease, 60–88. Washington, D.C.: Island Press.

Nabhan, Gary Paul. 2012. *Desert Terroir: Exploring the Unique Flavors and Sundry Places of the Borderlands.* Austin: University of Texas Press.

Nobel, Park S. 1982. "Spine Influences on PAR Interception, Stem Temperature, and Nocturnal Acid Accumulation in Cacti." *Plant, Cell and Environment* 6:153–59.

Ollerton, Jeff. 2006. "'Biological Barter': Patterns of Specialization Compared Across Different Mutualisms." In *Plant-Pollinator Interactions: From Specialization to Generalization,* edited by Nicolas Waser and Jeff Ollerton, 411–38. Chicago: University of Chicago Press.

Palermo, Elizabeth. 2013. "Why Does Rain Smell Good?" *Live Science,* June 21, 2013. https://www.livescience.com/37648-good-smells-rain-petrichor.html.

Pellmyr, Ollie. 2003. "Yuccas, Yucca Moths, and Coevolution: A Review." *Annals of the Missouri Botanical Garden* 90 (1): 35–55.

Pérez de Ribas, Andrés. 1968. *My Life Among the Savage Nations of New Spain.* Translated by Tomas Antonio Robertson. Los Angeles, CA: Ward Ritchie Press.

Powell, John Wesley. 1878. *Report on the Lands of the Arid Region of the United States.* Reprinted in 2004 as *Arid Lands* by the University of Nebraska Press, Lincoln.

Radding, Cynthia 1997. *Wandering Peoples: Colonialism, Ethnic Spaces, and Ecological Frontiers in Northwestern Mexico, 1700–1850.* Durham, NC: Duke University Press.

Raguso, Rob A., and Andre Kessler 2017. "Speaking in Chemical Tongues: Decoding the Language of Plant Volatiles." In *The Language of Plants: Science, Philosophy, Literature,* edited by Monica Gagliano, John C. Ryan, and Patrícia Vieira, 46–58. Minneapolis: University of Minnesota Press.

Sequín, Margareta. 2018. *The Chemistry of Plants: Perfumes, Pigments and Poisons*. London: Royal Society of Chemistry.

Sherbrooke, Wade C. 1990. "Rain-Harvesting in the lizard, *Phrynosoma cornutum*: Behavior and Integumental Morphology." *Journal of Herpetology* 24 (3): 302–8.

Shreve, Forrest. 1915. *Vegetation of a Desert Mountain Range*. Carnegie Institution of Washington, Publication 217. Washington, D.C.: Carnegie Institution.

Shreve, Forrest. 1951. *Vegetation of the Sonoran Desert*. Carnegie Institution of Washington, Publication 591. Washington, D.C.: Carnegie Institution.

Shryock, Andrew, Daniel Lord Smail, and Timothy Earle. 2011. *Deep History: The Architecture of Past and Present*. Berkeley: University of California Press.

Slack, Nancy. 2006. "Ecology Beginning with Botanists." *Science* 311 (5764): 1101–2.

Soule, Michael E., and Gary Lease. 1995. *Reinventing Nature? Responses to Post-Modern Deconstruction*. Washington D.C.: Island Press.

Stone, L., and A. Roberts. 1991. "Conditions for a Species to Gain Advantage from the Presence of Competitors." *Ecology* 72:1964–72.

Suzan-Azpiri, Humberto, Gary Paul Nabhan, and Duncan Patten. 1994. "Nurse Plant Ecology and Floral Biology of a Rare Night-Blooming Cereus Cactus, *Peniocereus striatus* (Brandegee) Buxbaum." *Conservation Biology* 8 (3): 461–70.

Suzan-Azpiri, Humberto, Gary Paul Nabhan, and Duncan Patten. 1996. "The Importance of *Olneya tesota* as a Nurse Plant in the Sonoran Desert." *Journal of Vegetation Science* 7:635–44.

Tewksbury, Joshua J., Gary Paul Nabhan, Don Norman, John Tuxill, and Jim Donavan. 1999. "In Situ Conservation of Wild Chiles and Their Biological Associates." *Conservation Biology* 131:98–107.

Tobey, R. C. 1981. *Saving the Prairies: The Life Cycle of the Founding School of American Plant Ecology, 1895–1955*. Berkeley: University of California Press.

Treutlein, Theodore, ed. and trans. 1989. *Ignaz Pfefferkorn's Sonora: A Description of a Province*. Tucson: University of Arizona Press.

van Beneden, Pierre J. 1873. *Animals and Their Mess-Mates*. London: Henry S. King.

Ward, David. 2012. "Desert Biome." *Oxford Bibliographies*, May 23, 2012. https://www.oxfordbibliographies.com/view/document/obo-9780199830060/obo-9780199830060-0044.xml.

Waser, Nick, and Leslie Real. 1979. "Effective Mutualism Between Sequentially Flowering Plant Species." *Nature* 281:670–72.

Weaver, J. E., and F. E. Clements. 1938. *Plant Ecology*. 2nd ed. New York: McGraw-Hill.

Went, Fritz. 1973. "Competition Among Plants." *Proceedings of the National Academy of Sciences* 70:585–90.

Wilder, Benjamin, and Carolyn O'Meara. 2015. "The Continuum of Desert Research." *Journal of the Southwest* 57 (2–3): 163–86.

Wilder, Judith C. 1967. "The Years of the Desert Laboratory." *Journal of Arizona History* 8 (3): 179–99.

Williams, George. 1966. *Adaptation and Natural Selection: A Critique of Some Current Evolutionary Thought*. Princeton, NJ: Princeton University Press.

Withgott, Jay. 2000. "Botanical Nursing." *BioScience* 50:479–84.

Worster, Donald. 1994. *Nature's Economy: A History of Ecological Ideas*. New York: Oxford University Press.

NATIVE WAYS OF ENVISIONING DESERTS

WHERE THE WILDERNESS BEGINS

OFELIA ZEPEDA

Perhaps, when it really was not necessary, since there was no one else around when the Creator formed the shape of the first human and was about to place him on the ground, he ran his hand across the spot where the human was going to be put. Perhaps the place cleared was only the size of the human's feet, or perhaps the space was the size of the state of Texas; surely he must have signified a space.

As children we have done the same. I remember playing on the cool earth floor on a hot summer day, and even though the dirt surface that was our yard and play area had been designated by our mother, we defined it further. Her signal to the space was to sprinkle it with water and sweep it every morning in order to keep the surface firm and dust free. The dirt floor was hard as cement. Once we sat down on it, whether we were playing jacks, dolls, or cars, we further ran our hands over a certain spot on this floor, clearing it and designating it as where we would play. We cleared a small space for the rag dolls to sleep. We cleared further spaces that featured roads or served as places for houses and other childhood toys. We redefined space that was already ours.

Living in the desert, we have all done the same. We have marked the space within the space that is already ours. This space, I say, is already ours, ours in the sense that this is our habitat: we are the ones who were put here to live. And even though we live here, we continue to remark it, create boundaries. We fence in, and out. We know where the "wild" desert ends and the "other space" begins. Now because we know where the desert ends, we also know *what* is in that desert. Sometimes we know these things firsthand, sometimes not. As O'odham, we know the desert is the place of wilderness. It is the place of dreams for those who must dream those kinds of dreams, and it is the place of songs for those who must sing those kinds of songs. But it is also the place where nightmares hide, nightmares so fierce that one can believe one has seen a guardian angel. For the O'odham, the desert is certainly a place of power. Because we know this essence of the desert, although sometimes we do not fully understand it, we are able to live in it.

In talking about living in the desert, I will hold some of the perspective of the Tohono O'odham, the Desert People, a tribe indigenous to the southern Arizona desert. I will pull from what I know personally, some of it certainly gained along the way from family. Other things that I say are bits of other O'odham people's stories.

As a child I grew up knowing two communities, communities that complemented each other very well. Much of my childhood was spent in the place I was born, Stanfield, Arizona. Stanfield was a cotton-farming community up until the early '70s. This community was a desert region, but with a new façade, a façade of greenery pushed up from the ground artificially. Despite its appearance, this place still had limited rainfall with the regular urgency of summer monsoons. The temperatures were extreme, the air dry and clear. The winters were the same as in any desert, mildly cold and tolerable.

The other place was a village just inside the Mexican border, which was my mother's traditional home. When I was a child, our family spent time there, too. This place was also an agricultural region of sorts. It was noted for its numerous natural springs and, at that time, its large surface ponds. We planted fields mostly of corn, melon, squash, and beans. There were also orchards of pomegranates and figs. This village was an oasis, and so special it was considered by some as a sacred place. From these two homelands in the desert, I grew up familiar with it and knowing how to live in it. Even though both places were clearly defined by their water and agricultural boundaries, in both places one did not need to look too far to see where the "wild desert" began.

It began at the end of the cotton fields or just over a low hill. It was beyond these places, the ends of the fields and over desert hills, that we as children knew not to venture too far. I remember adults telling us, "Something is going to get you" should we venture toward those desert regions. These threats were not false threats of the bogeyman; no, they were real. It was the case then, as it is now, that members of society who do not fit elsewhere often-times find themselves on the edges of communities, in the desert, existing as well as they can. It was these people that adults warned us against. Another thing to fear is something that we cannot see but believe exists. "Something is going to get you" sometimes referred, not to anything physical, but to something psychological or spiritual. O'odham believe that one can be met by a being, a spirit, at almost any time. These meetings can happen in the most mundane places, but they can also occur in more mystical wilderness areas like the desert. And unless one actually ventures out for such a meeting because one is supposed to, it is best to keep one's chances low by avoiding the mystical places, the wilderness spaces, whenever possible.

There is a story about a male relative who after a night of partying and drinking ended up having to walk home the next day. His walk put him in the midst of dry, wild desert for a considerable stretch. The story goes that he suffered dehydration, not to mention mild sunstroke coupled with hangover, and in this state, he had a meeting with a spirit animal. The animal he claims to have met was the bear who gave him songs. My mother tells this story with some humor. She asks, where would a bear come from? It does not live in that desert. Nonetheless, this relative had the songs. Unfortunately, he did not live very long, and as far as anyone knows never had a single opportunity to take advantage of his curing power on anyone suffering sickness caused by the bear—perhaps it was just as well.

There are many accounts of O'odham men who have been called to go out in the desert for such meetings. These meetings are for gaining knowl-edge about a variety of traditional ways, including curing rituals, songs, and finding solutions to various major concerns, either for themselves or for the group. As children we were kept vaguely informed about such goings-on. On occasion if we asked too many questions, we were simply given the explana-tion that so and so went hunting and that was the reason for being gone for several days at a time. Even in our cottonfield town, we knew of men who went out into the desert because they were supposed to. I remember watching them walk down the road alongside the cottonfield, come to the end of the field, turn away, and disappear into the desert. The desert does hold all sorts of power, much of it not accessible to everyone, most of it harmless.

There are other stories from out of the desert that have nearly become folklore among many O'odham. One such story tells of something that exists in certain parts of the desert. This thing they speak of is not a physical being, and it has been ascertained by those knowledgeable that it is not a spiritual being either. And the features of this thing? Well, it has none, none yet described by anyone, since no one has really seen it. Those who have experienced this phenomenon claim it is an air, a feeling, and when one gets too close to such a place one experiences the basest, most visceral fear an evolved human is capable of. People tell how a horse will not go near an area that manifests this thing; they sense a fear unlike any other, according to those who know horses. This is a phenomenon that some people like to tell about with much relish and exaggerated detail. Some dismiss it as the bogeyman syndrome, while others are convinced this thing is truly a manifestation of Satan himself. Whether any of this is true is still in question.

Those who do not believe might perhaps think differently when they hear Mrs. Antone's story. What she saw caused her to be so overcome by such fear that the only thing that saved her from being scared out of her wits was a beautiful vision of what she believed to be a guardian angel. This experience led her to relocate to a bigger cleared space in the desert, become a born-again Christian, and join the Assembly of God church.

She tells her story:

I had just gotten married. I married a Mexican man. We were both young. This was around 1940, back when there was no electricity in the desert. Anyway, he took me to his home. It was just a little shack out in the middle of the desert. There were no other houses near us. We were alone except for a few of his cows. It was nighttime when we got to his place, and it was really dark, no moon. We had only been there a short time when he suddenly said he had to leave. I didn't want him to leave because I didn't want to stay there alone. He told me, "Take this and you will be all right." He handed me his .22 and left. I didn't know what to do. I started to go about the little house and straighten up, trying to keep my mind off being alone.

Suddenly, I heard something outside. At first it was like a breeze blowing through, maybe a little dust devil. But when I quickly looked outside, none of the tree limbs were moving. As I stood in the middle of that little house, I felt this thing move the walls of the house just slightly, and as suddenly as it had begun, it stopped. And then I had a sensation something was inside the house with me. It was like cold, wet air. It seemed to permeate my being. I don't know how to explain it. I know it seemed to possess me because it seemed it was holding me not the same way a man or a woman would hold another with the arms, but it held me on the inside of my body, by my backbone. I couldn't move, I couldn't feel my skin, I couldn't breathe even though I was alive. Have you ever seen someone take their last breath before they die and their blood stops running through their body? I think I felt my blood stop running. I felt dry, not wet and alive the way a human is supposed to. I stood there and just held my .22 rifle to my chest. My mind, I don't know what my mind was doing. It was either not working or it was working too fast to be of any use. Thoughts were running all around, too many, too quickly, like a bag full of marbles spilled on a concrete floor. I searched quickly, my mind. The only thing I recall was something that told me to pray. That is all. So I did. I prayed and prayed and prayed for what seemed like an eternity. That was all my mind could do. Finally, *It* released me. I felt my fingers warm up with the rush of blood. I could move. The first thing I did was look out this little hole in the door into the blackness, and I saw something floating. It was white. It floated above the house and upward until I couldn't see it anymore. It was like one of those beautiful angels I used to see in the books. Then I understood what it was—my guardian angel. It was my guardian angel that had come and saved me from that thing. I just know this is what happened.

When Mrs. Antone told me her story, she was living in a small Arizona town, which of course was in the desert but had been altered by the pumping of underground water, irrigated fields, and copper mining.

I began by stating that O'odham, to a certain extent, know how to live in the desert because, to a certain extent, they know what is in that desert. Some of it is good, and some not. Some of it is real, and some perhaps manufactured by active imaginations. Regardless, contemporary O'odham have available to them various insurance options they can "purchase" in order to protect the space they have set up as their homes within the desert. One option is a cleared yard and a fence, which primarily acts as a deterrent to medium-sized wild animals. The cleared yard is often a meeting ground for uninvited animals, where their host has the option of redirecting the animal back to its original trail. The fence and yard, though, are no match for the more spirit-formed intruder. The option in this case for many O'odham is to invite the local medicine man over to "clean" the house and space. This cleaning protects the building and space from nonphysical intrusions. And for many O'odham who may also happen to be Catholic, a double dose of spiritual protection can come in the form of the local padre who can, following the medicine man, "bless" the space and the house. Finally, some families may have a fiesta at their home. Part of the fiesta might include ritual dancing by the neighboring Yoeme—either Matachine dancing or, even better, Deer Dancing. This dancing offers protection insurance because wherever the Matachines dance, the ground becomes sacred; the same is true for the Deer Dancer, but with the Deer Dancer is the additional bonus of the holy water from the gourd drum. Once the celebration is completed, the water from the drum is sprinkled all about, and the place is holy—to some, sacred. I have a friend who does not allow cars in the parking space next to his house because that is where the dancers danced. Even he has to park his truck out on the street.

So there we are. To live in the desert is to know the desert as well as possible, and if that is not the case, then there certainly are ways to protect oneself.

HEENO

ALBERTO MELLADO MORENO

eeno (*monte* in Spanish, *desert* or *brush* in English) is what the Comcáac, or Seri, community have called me for millennia. *Heeno* or *hehe án* are the names they gave me, for I am a dry wild place full of plants, away from where most humans congregate. I have been here for more time than anyone can record, even the Comcáac. They are among indigenous peoples who came to me from other places so long ago that the year of their arrival is incalculable.

Nevertheless, they have made me part of their families, and they, mine. They have wrapped the fibers of my plants around their naked feet. For thousands of years now they have placed their bare feet on my sun-baked skin and wandered high and low.

Sometimes they have briefly left me to enter the sea that lay by my side. Ever since they first waded into the waters, I have watched while they launched their little kayak-like boats. These boats they made from carrizo canes lashed into bundles, using canes that they cut and selected for their buoyancy on the edge of deep springs that well up in my crevices.

When the Comcáac first arrived, they told me of my own origins; they told me I was created by Hant Caai—just like they were too. I told them of my origins, and they too said that they were formed by Hant Caai—the Creator of all life.

At one time I was part of that hot mass that was the earth when it first appeared. But I was not yet alive. My sisters, the other lands of the earth, and I were sleeping in the depths of the seas, under all that water, until the power of Hant Caai had us open our eyes and wake up in the depths of the seas and rise up until we reached the surface.

That was how it was until the supernatural powers of Hant Caai allowed us to open our eyes, awakening in the bottom of the sea. We departed from that primordial place and rose until we emerged on the surface of this earth.

When all my relations who emerged with me and I suddenly felt the fresh air on our skin, we realized that we had come above the water for the first time ever. Hant Caai transformed some of us into islands surrounded by seas, while he reformed others into large masses of land.

That is when the Comcáac informed me that the Creator, in the form of Hant Hasóoma, had placed plants and animals all around us. Then, in the form of an old man named Cmaacoj Cmaasol, he came into this world on his own to wander across my skin. He did this to give names to all that had come into existence by that time. He gave each of the plants a power we call *hehe*, which makes them grow, alter the weather, or heal our wounds. As he raced through the desert naming the plants, his skin became coated with the golden pollen from creosote bushes; that is why we thought of him as a yellow-colored man (Cmaacoj Cmaasol). And in that time, he taught the names of the flora and fauna to the Comcáac, giving them a unique language that I now speak as well.

Hant Hasóoma as Cmaacoj Cmaasol gave the Comcáac a special name for me, for since the beginning of time, they have affectionately called me Heeno.

My sisters and brothers and I were born with different skins. Two of them have whitish skin, made of moisture and stone frozen together into a solid mass. One of these two pale bodies became a kind of star that never moves from its place on the horizon, while the other one sits near the horizon in the opposite direction. Between these two pale luminaries, the sun comes up and then disappears each and every day.

Others of my brothers and sisters live closer to me. One of my brothers is now very tall, and his skin has formed into steep cliffs of sheer slickrock, with a few spindly pine trees that reach high above us. Other relations of mine have greener bodies, made verdant by virtue of the lush growth of trees and the copious flow of water.

And yet, I am distinct among all my relations, for I have grown a skin of sand and stone, of plants with spines and thorns, of leaflets small but fragrant, of miniscule pools of water that sparkle like gems in the sun. Together, we form something altogether different, a place easily distinguished from all the rest.

In fact, I have always felt full of life; I have always felt as if I have had all I need, for the Comcáac had taught the names and use of every plant and animal that lives on my skin. Hant Hasóoma—the spirit of the driest wildlands—showed them how we can be nourished by the gum of the jumping cholla. Searching my body for crevices and cavities, they also discovered plenty of water, even though it had been hidden from others.

With their stunning capacity to come to know me in every way, they handed over to their children this precious knowledge. They would arrive in a place and soon encounter water where no one else had recorded it, for they knew that I would keep it just below my skin in places where no one else had looked.

The Comcáac were also the ones who told me that the Creator could simply glance at my mountains and carve into them into caves full of power. These caves held a kind of supernatural power that he would pass on to them during rites of passage that transformed certain persons into the most extraordinary men and women of their community.

Over our time together, they made me realize what an incalculable quantity and diversity of life has gathered around us. Where the sands of my body became edged or submerged by the sea, the Comcáac became skilled hunters of sea turtles, of the giant fish called *totoaba*, of other classes of fish, crabs, clams, oysters, and scallops that are good to eat.

With the passage of time, they turned me into part of their community, and they became part of me. From the most ancient times, whenever the Comcáac lost their lives, they were put to rest beneath my skin, for they were given to me to safeguard forever, so that I could care for them to keep the memory of them alive. At the same time, the mothers of newborn babies buried their placentas beneath my skin.

From the earth where they are buried, I have let the roots of plants that they would soon eat grow up out my skin, so they could be nourished. While the silenced bodies of their ancients and their spent placentas may have seemed stilled, they intertwined with the feet of the plants that have continued to walk through time. No one could detain or contain these lives as separate beings. In this manner, I came to know that part of me belonged to each of them, and part of them to me.

Eventually, the Comcáac budded off into families, clans, and bands that spread out across my body to live in different habitats—some on the edge of the sea, others in the middle of islands, still others along arroyos that ran down from the hills far from the ocean. So many of them planted their placentas, as well as *antepasados*, within all parts of my body that we nearly came to be one and the same.

As time passed, we came to know one another's gifts and needs. I was able to help them as much as I could by planting in my skin powerful plants such as saguaros that can always bear fruit to eat each summer. In other seasons, I would alert them when the fish, crabs, and scallops became ready to harvest on the edge of the sea where they congregated.

In the shallow sand banks in the bays where my body was submerged, I would let the beds of eelgrass grow up from me like hair on my body, so that the various kinds of sea turtles could seek them out close to where the Comcáac camped. I made sure that they would always have turtles from the sea for their feasts and their ceremonies. I made sure the deer could run free from the dry hills of the interior to the wetter edges of my body, where the waves washed up on the beaches.

After each rainfall, I would gather and guard all the water I could offer them, preserving it in the shady canyons between rocky ridges, and in the succulence of trees and other plants, where the heat would have a harder time forcing it to evaporate into thin air. I found ways to let the rivers and streams carve openings in my skin where the water could drain underground to where the Comcáac camped, near artesian springs and upwellings of sweet water just above the ocean's salt edge. I would also keep watch over the storm waters that filled up charcos and other small ponds that had been dug.

These reservoirs smeared mud onto my skin and left enough fine clay behind that the Comcáac could make eggshell-thin pottery vessels to hold water for their families during times of drought.

Some years the rains did not come at all, so the people coaxed water out of the roots of cholla cactus to survive. In other years, the torrential rains of hurricanes suddenly arrived. I had to protect the Comcáac from these downpours, and from the searing rays of the sun. I taught them to take refuge in coastal lagoons shielded by mangroves or in caves shielded by the mountains during such hard times.

But then—one day about five hundred years ago—other kinds of men came across the seas from faraway lands. They began to massacre the Comcáac and the other neighboring tribes in the desert. This genocide was unlike anything that had occurred for thousands of years, for I had to receive under my skin thousands of corpses of my family and friends. At the same time, few new placentas were being placed within me.

My body carried the burden of all those who had lost their lives to war or to diseases introduced from afar. I tried so hard to help the Comcáac in their war of resistance against these perverse strangers, concealing them in my mountains and canyons, or helping them take refuge far out on the islands, but ultimately, I simply could not save all whom I wished to protect.

The foreigners who came from other lands knew nothing of the desert; they pierced my skin with a chain of crosses, where they built churches, haciendas, and towns. They made new wounds in my body to allow the passage of *carretas* and wagons, pulled by the strange animals they called horses, oxen, mules, and donkeys, which they treated as slaves.

They insinuated themselves into every cavity, molesting every pit and orifice in my body in search for nuggets of gold, silver, or precious metals. When they found traces of these riches, they then dug into my body, injecting into it a toxic liquid called *azogue*, or mercury, to concentrate the minerals they mined from me.

The Comcáac fought them with bows and arrows, but the firearms their enemies fired would explode with a thunderous sound and power that tore at their bodies, drenching them in their own blood.

The invaders placed all over my body the livestock they brought from other countries. These horses and oxen pulled plows that tore open my skin so that the foreigners could sow what they called their cultivated crops. But in doing so, they pulled down mesquite trees, saguaros, chollas, and shrubs, ripping their roots from my skin.

I had to protect the remaining Comcáac on the biggest island away from the mainland, so that the invaders would not exterminate them. But only a small portion of them remained alive, fewer than two hundred individuals. This made my heart sad, especially when their enemies removed the corpses and placentas I had tried to keep safe under my skin. They diverted water from all the rivers, using it to irrigate their crops.

Those were difficult times for us, and the only surviving record that we had was the rock art in the caves and on rock walls that they made on my skin, using the same symbols that they have always painted on their faces to express our identity.

The newly arrived peoples destroyed me little by little, but the remaining Comcáac still took refuge where they could find small seeps or springs of water in the deserts and mountains. Their descendants became cautious and secretive but still knew our distinctive language and culture. There they would occasionally find others of our kind, just one or two survivors, or more rarely, a small group of relatives that knew our distinctive language and culture. There they would offer to protect me, to clean and wash my wounds.

Among the new generation of Comcáac were descendants of the most powerful individuals, whom no one could kill. They persisted with our ways, adapted to this place, and when they left their refuges on the island, they resettled a few places on the mainland that had been the homes of their ancestors. They gathered together to repatriate and concentrate in a small area where they would no longer be isolated from one another.

One part of me felt that I had been saved when they began to dance again on my skin, and when their hands touch my sands. With great joy, I saw them grow in number year after year, and even though their placentas were no longer offered to me to absorb, their roots continued to reach deep within me again. I knew that as long as they continued to live, I too would exist, until the last of them takes a handful of my earth and tosses it up toward the new moon, just as the very first time we encountered one another thousands of years ago.

I COMMIT TO MEMORY THE DESERT VILLAGE, MY FAMILY, AND MY HOME

OCTAVIANA V. TRUJILLO

I was born in an adobe home in the Yaqui village of Guadalupe, behind the cultural plaza during a cold night two days after Christmas. Guadalupe is one of at least six villages of the Yoeme, or Yaqui, people in the Arizona reach of the Sonoran Desert, and the only one that has survived the expansion of Metro Phoenix. My parents had built our small four-room house there out of the local earth, making adobes out of the clay, sand, and dried plant matter they gleaned from the still-open spaces that surrounded the village.

I was raised in this desert home with seven brothers and three sisters. It is where we grew up and learned about the world. I was named in honor of our grandmother, Octaviana Vacasequa, who would come to our home almost every day. Our grandmother spoke Yoeme, Spanish, and English, but her English was limited since she had attended only a few years of school. My grandmother learned some additional English when she worked with the Works Progress Administration (WPA) program during the Great Depression.

Octaviana was a fast walker, and sometimes I would try to keep up with her as she would go around the village. She visited with many of our neighbors, for she served as the primary translator in our village when people needed such assistance. Many families in our village did not trust outsiders, so they sought out my grandmother whenever they needed a sympathetic go-between.

My grandmother was also a traditional healer, social worker, legal counsel, and oral historian. She played so many roles that were needed in a small desert village like ours. I would shadow my grandmother as her companion on her many visits to other families in the village. I admired how she listened and gave serious thought to how to solve the problem at hand. As I listened to the ways she found good resolutions to most issues, I realized that she was not just my grandmother but my best teacher as well.

Like most others in Guadalupe at that time, my parents would walk out into the surrounding desert at least once a week to collect mesquite, the primary fuel for our wood-burning stoves. Because of the sweet fragrance of its smoke, the whole village was laden with a pleasant aroma.

I still love many of the fragrances I associate with our desert village. Sometimes I would go outside our home and, with our dipper, splash water on the adobe wall. I would take in a whiff of it and, on occasion, even taste its damp earthen soil.

All the homes in our village were made the same way and carried that same earthy aroma. Early in the morning, mothers and grandmothers would dampen the clay floors to make them firm, so that they would release a minimum of dust.

As children, we would gather up some food—usually the surplus commodities that the government dumped on us—and load them up in our little homemade cart. We would then pull our cart over to our own special dwelling place, a mile or so west of the village. There, hidden back in Pima Canyon and out of view of Metro Phoenix, we had claimed a miniature village of casitas—little structures made of dry stone walls. Very few outsiders would go there, so we had the desert canyon to ourselves most of the time. Later in life, I learned that the WPA had built them.

Along the way to our casitas, we would stop at the Fray Marcos de Niza stone inscription. Now and then, we would see on the trail all sorts of desert creatures: roadrunners, coyotes, desert tortoises, Gila monsters, jackrabbits, and sometimes snakes. Often, we would build a small campfire near the casitas to pretend we were "camping" like the kids we saw on TV.

Since our village was in the desert, we could use many of the trees and herbs that were part of our way of life and ceremonies. My grandmother would collect the "greasy" branches of *hediondilla* from the creosote plants for medicinal use. (*Hediondilla* means "little stinker" in Spanish, for it was so aromatic it could expel bugs and germs.) The men in the village would also go into the desert to cut wood, building ramadas for our homes and fiestas with viga crossbeams and upright posts of mesquite trunks.

During the ceremonies for the Day of the Holy Cross, old crosses were burned, and new ones made from the willow tree were placed on our doors. Every spring, our ceremonies were held at the top of a little hill called Santa Cruz, not far from our village. Now this little hill has a restaurant at the top and interstate highway next to it. Would we say that it has been desecrated, that it is no longer sacred?

Sacred objects come and go. Like some of the masks used in our ceremonies, the old willow crosses that adorned the entrances to our homes were burned, and the new crosses made to replace them were decorated with crepe paper flowers. Some of the young village boys would get overly excited and would start burning the branches of other desert trees. By the time the darkness of the evening came, one could see small short-lived fires brightening the hillsides of Santa Cruz. These controlled burns were probably a good thing, for the branches of desert shrubs would resprout to be much healthier and greener in the aftermath of these brushfires.

Our ceremonies are dependent on our access to and care for so many desert plants and animals. They have become vital elements in our culture.

On my first trip to our eight sacred pueblos in our ancient homeland, along the Río Yaqui in Sonora, I was taken into the desert to collect the dried thorny fruit of the gigantic columnar cacti we collectively refer to as pitaya. Reyna, a Yaqui woman from Potam, was my mentor. She showed me how to burn off the ends of the thorny fruit so that it could be used as a hairbrush. (Its scientific name commemorates this indigenous use: *Pachycereus pecten-aboriginum*.)

And so our ancient traditions of the desert live on to this day. Reyna's husband, Blas, told us how the desert still gives us everything: food, drink, medicine, shelter, and protection—and ultimately, the distinctiveness of our way of life. Our rituals are also dependent on desert plants and animals, as the Yaqui Deer and Pascola ceremonial dances attest. These rituals remind us what gives life to us.

Since leaving Guadalupe after spending my entire youth there, I have been blessed to travel to other deserts abroad: the Negev, Sahara, Atacama, and many more. Each time I begin to take the long journey back home, however, I feel this longing for my desert welling up in me.

From the airplane window, I see the body of my homelands: the sacred mountain ranges, fertile valleys, deep arroyos and canyons, and the green markings along the rivers of the cottonwoods, willows, palo verdes, saguaros, mesquites, and creosote bushes.

My sense of smell is once again aroused. My sensory pleasure of being in the desert again spills over into feelings of and tastes of joy as I return to what is most familiar and fully embrace the desert that has been my home. I am overcome with *querencia*, the yearning for the fragrances, flavors, textures, and tastes I associate with the homelands of my childhood.

GROWING UP
DESERTED

A SENSE OF PLACE AND A SENSE OF SELF

The Acquisition of Compassion from the Desert

PAUL DAYTON

"Paulie, just try to see the world through his eyes." This was my mother's wisdom as I struggled through my dyslexic childhood dealing with school bullies and scary bits of nature. I spent my formative years in the Sonoran Desert and then logging camps in the Oregon woods, where I learned to empathize with the animals rather than fear them. It offered a lifetime lesson that served me well when the family moved back to our roots in Tucson, Arizona, where my mother's wisdom took hold as I explored the desert alone and with Eli, my competent and sympathetic brother. As the catclaws ripped my clothes and skin, and the agaves along the Pusch Ridge in upper Pima Canyon bloodied my legs, I realized that they were protecting themselves.

They were not enemies but other organisms simply trying to live their lives in peace. I easily understood that the spiny cacti, rattlesnakes, scorpions, and other venomous animals were also protecting themselves, and I learned to appreciate their problems from their perspective. When the black widow spider bit me as I squashed her in my bed, I felt sorry for the spider.

Over the years as I wandered around the Sonoran Desert, trying to see through the evolutionary eyes of the plants and animals, I developed a genuine sense of place, in which I realized that these rugged organisms thrived in many cases as a result of a tangled web of mutualistic interactions. For example, it was easy to understand the role of a legume (usually a palo verde or sometimes a mesquite) with deep tap roots nursing a saguaro, how the limbs supported the bird that shat the seeds, how the overstory protected the tiny cacti from both sunburn and freezing, and how the nitrogen-fixing bacteria cultivated by the legume fed the young cacti via the litter the tree produced.

I learned how hydraulic lift resulting from daytime evapotranspiration dried out the shallow roots and soil, and at night osmotic pressures brought water from the deeper roots up into the dried surface area, bringing moisture to the small cacti and other plants beneath the nurse tree.

I would sit under the nurse tree watching the pollinators at work. I learned that some, such as the tarantula hawk (a wasp), also depended on killing my beloved tarantulas, which were necessary to feed their young. When in flower, the nurse tree attracted clouds of dragonflies that hawked the pollinators. I learned that the beetles that killed the legumes seeds were often parasitized by a wasp.

Slowly I watched the cactus that had been so well nursed grow large enough to compete with the legume for water, sometimes stressing the legume such that it was vulnerable to mistletoe, which usually killed the nurse plant, leaving the saguaro alone or in a cluster with no hint of the nurse tree.

Or, if the nurse tree was lucky, its branches touched the saguaro, and sometimes a packrat chewed big chunks of the cactus, leaving the sap vulnerable to fruit flies and other insects, which sometimes brought a disease that killed the cactus and spared the nurse tree. I realized that the presence or absence of these vectors depended on rainfall, and that they, as well as the packrat populations, cycled with significant lag periods following the rain.

By observing and thinking through their eyes, I became sympathetic to the jumping cholla, the bane of desert hikers. They are triploid and reproduce asexually by dropping *joints*, which are mostly eaten by packrats. The joints, or vegetative buds, tend to be produced one to two years after wet winters, which reflect the two- to five-year El Niño cycles. The pulse of cholla buds stimulates the packrat populations with another lag period of one to two years.

The packrats then created other mischief, such as chewing on the saguaro. But I also saw chollas nurse several species of plants, including ocotillo and palo verde seedlings, by protecting them from black-tailed jackrabbits.

Unlike the legumes, the cholla have shallow root systems, vulnerable to competition with the plants that they protect, and the cholla lose the competition for moisture and die, leaving healthy ocotillo and palo verde, which might survive to facilitate all the other species it will feed with its nectar and foliage.

The desert has taught me patience, as I observe seed banks germinate only once in more than forty years after an effective rain event. At the same time, I learned that theretofore unsuspected huge roots of *Marah gilensis*, the coyote cucumber vine, were alive and well, common if unseen below ground over decades, awaiting the unusual rain after which they flourished, growing on and over and sometimes even killing senita, saguaro, and creosote bushes.

With all the growth, species of butterflies and other insects not seen in decades showed up and lived out their life cycles. I observed a large Sonoran Desert toad apparently living out the dry years in mammal burrows and coming out after a wet period attempting to ambush pocket mice, as well as a red spotted toad stalking insects. Both amphibians were miles from any water, and they patiently persevered in underground safe spots during the normal heat and dryness.

This kaleidoscope of interactions through space and time has profoundly influenced my own sense of self and has given me the perspective my mother attempted to offer so long ago. These complex interactions seen through the eyes of the organisms successfully surviving in a harsh environment force an appreciation of the complex interactions that individuals and societies experience in their own dynamic spheres.

They teach us the necessity of cooperation and self-defense; of patience, self-confidence, and humility; and, maybe most of all, a sense of empathy and compassion for all the organisms in both the natural and human systems we experience.

MY CHILDHOOD DESERT

ALBERTO BÚRQUEZ

Until I was a teenager, I took for granted the desert's marvels and its grandeur. I grew up in the open spaces. My childhood days were filled with fun in the desert hills, in the sandy dry arroyos, and along the arid seashore. In my forays into the wilds, I harvested pitaya fruits and scoured the desert for prized flint arrowheads, for eggshell pottery of ancient Comcáac (Seri) Indians, and for hidden, unknown treasures. Like most parents of baby boomers, mine were caring and watchful but at times oblivious to our safety, allowing us to roam in the desert for hours on end with temperatures 110°+F.

Against all odds, I managed to survive. I discovered that the desert is a multidimensional place that inspires awe, terror, and, to some, the unbearable desire to transform it. Later in life, I found countless volumes describing the desert: paperbacks with pen drawings of cacti and lizards; coffee table books with splendid colorful images; scholarly treatises full of graphs, maps, and equations; art books with Georgia O'Keeffe's mountains and flowers; engineering and agronomical books promising, always in vain, to turn the desert into a lush green paradise.

After a long trip on horseback through the Sonoran Desert, the New York art historian and critic John Van Dyke penned, "the desert should never be reclaimed!" And yet, by the December 1911 issue of the *Plant World*—a magazine edited by Tucson's Desert Laboratory director Forrest Shreve—readers were invited to purchase pumping machinery for "reclaiming desert lands" from the local mercantile, Albert Steinfeld and Company. While Van Dyke's writing became a best seller known as *The Desert*, and the *Plant World* turned into the prestigious journal *Ecology*, those set on reclaiming the desert were not dissuaded from it by the eloquence of Van Dyke and Shreve.

More than one hundred years later, vast expanses of desert have been developed, thanks to the construction of large dams and canals, the exploitation of deep aquifers, and the incessant flow of cheap energy from oil, all used to propel industrial agribusiness. For many, they still see a desert as a "clean slate" for new development. The desert's Achilles heel lies in its delicate ecological balance and fragile structure.

My grandfather had a photograph of a hunting party in which three fat Sonoran pronghorn antelopes lay on the hood of a dusty Packard. The car is absurdly parked in an open plain among creosote bushes, not far from La Noria Verde, where Van Dyke signed the preface of his book. Now, the herds of antelope Van Dyke wrote about, and the pure dry air that lured him to the desert to treat his asthma, are long gone.

Still, vast expanses of land, millions of acres of silent desert hold secrets, marvels, and a diverse landscape with unique animals and plants, west of La Noria Verde, at a place called El Fin del Mundo, in the Vizcaíno region of Baja California, and in the Gran Desierto de Altar.

For the mystics among us, these sanctuaries remain sacred places. For the artist, the desert remains a place of communion with the silence, the crisp transparency of the air, the play of lights, and the rugged backdrop of distant mountains. It is more than the sum of its parts, a whole harboring an extraordinary biological and aesthetic diversity.

To speak of true deserts is to speak in hyperbole. They remain among the most fantastical environments on earth, with their plants and animals adhering to an elegant water economy.

We come to love their austere aridity, their bone-piercing spurts of cold winter air, their deluges that briefly drown out the drought, and their heat waves that can crack the skin, burn the lungs, and turn blood into fine sand.

Deserts come in all flavors, but all share the fantastic natural erosion patterns of rocks; the extensive alluvial fans; the dry rivers, arroyos, and wadis of intricate denditic geometry; the air of absolute transparency, with crisp shadows at noon that seem cut with knives; the skies that span a gamut of blues; the sunsets of gold and cinnabar that slowly turn into firefly-encrusted obsidian, with loud leagues of silence.

Our imaginations are left to play and stray in the silence, among the debris flows of rocks and the open skies.

Deserts were barely inhabited until rather recently in geological history, and only then by people as scarce as the few precious resources they hold. Nevertheless, the diversity of strategies for desert living found among indigenous peoples is astonishing. I am referring to the lifeways of the following cultures: the Berbers and Bedouins of the North African sands; the Warlpiri and Pitjantjatara of the Central Australlian desert; the O'odham and Comcáac of the Sonoran Desert; the prehistoric Peruvians of the Nazca coastal desert, who made impossibly large geomorphic intaglio figures; the nomadic descendants of Genghis Khan, who still roam Mongolia; the Druse, Kurds, and Swamp Arabs of Asia Minor; and the Khoisan dwellers of Namibia.

Paradoxically, several deserts served as the earliest cradles of agricultural civilization. In them, long-gone ancient cultures developed: the Hohokam, the Anasazi, the Nabateans, the Sumerians, and the Egyptians. At the same time, in Australia's driest outback, the Aborigines—one of the earliest and longest continuous foraging cultures that eschewed farming—precariously cling.

Deserts have fabled cities of gold: in Baghdad, in Khara, in Nazca, and in Cíbola. Lost treasures in the ever-moving sand, in deep chasms, in enchanted caves, in missions of unknown geography, like the Santa Bárbara mission of Father Kino, which vanished in the Gran Desierto.

All this is to tell you that I have slowly learned to appreciate the heterogeneity of deserts, and to appreciate the majesty of arid landscapes that cannot be described as simple collections of plants, animals, or rocks. They are often mystical places that transcend their biology and geology, where the doors of perception can seemingly be cleansed by contemplation.

Deserts are full of real wonders, rich history, and remarkable interactions between creatures. But in an effort to bring order to nature, some people see the southwestern American deserts as a Looney Tunes abstraction of barren landscapes, with Monument Valley rock formations and the odd saguaro-like cactus. To complete the picture, the fauna is mainly composed of an absurdly long-legged roadrunner and a long-nosed coyote. Its diversity amounts to two, sometimes three animal species. The entire flora of a Looney Tunes desert appears to be limited to just a couple of gangly plant species.

In contrast, the real Sonoran Desert and its higher elevation companion, the Chihuahuan Desert, are the most diverse reservoirs of flora and fauna in the drylands of North America, each with hundreds of unique animals and plants. These two deserts are north-south corridors of arid-adapted biodiversity bisected by a momentary "line in the sand"—an international boundary line that is like a fleeting mirage when measured by nature's own clock.

Hope Jahren has written that "a cactus doesn't live in the desert because it likes the desert; it lives there because the desert hasn't killed it yet."

Although powerful, her quotation about the desert is clearly the reflection of someone who has not yet found a way to feel relaxed in extreme desert environments. She seems happier in the microcosm of the closed spaces of the lab, as her compelling book *Lab Girl* clearly states. Through the eyes of a native Sonoran Desert dweller, it is more likely that "a cactus lives in the desert because it is a comfy paradise that fits it well. Living elsewhere will kill it."

RECONCILING COOPERATION VS. COMPETITION AMONG DESERT CREATURES

RAY PIEROTTI

As a young boy, growing up in the high desert around Albuquerque, I used to spend many hours wandering through the sage and chamisa. It always struck me that the lizards I searched for were likely to be found more often under these plants than any other, especially during the heat of the day.

I had been raised by my mother and grandmother to think of these iconic shrubs as the "watchers of the desert," because of their long life spans, their ability to warn other plants in their understories of danger from grazers, and their nurse-like provision of habitats for other species, including birds and mammals.

My youthful passion for wandering among other lifeforms in the desert led me toward a career in biology, where my mentors taught me that competition within and among species was more important than cooperation.

And yet, perhaps I was predisposed to see cooperation as a strong influence because of my peculiar upbringing surrounded by so many floral neighbors in the high desert. Over nearly fifty years as an evolutionary ecologist, I came to realize that cooperation and competition can basically be seen as two sides of the same coin; the presence of one makes the other inevitable.

This nondualistic reality is most clearly observed in life histories that involve multiple offspring living together in the same home ground as their parents. There, individuals function both as the closest of companions and the bitterest of rivals. The simultaneity of amity and enmity is simply an inescapable aspect of the complexity subsumed within the concept of sociality.

Even the apparently cooperative, even altruistic, act of a mother producing milk for her offspring generates a competitive context. Anyone who has observed a young fawn vigorously butting its mother's belly and teats to obtain access to the latter will note the intergenerational conflict involved. When resources are limited, there is scramble competition for available sources of food. When faced with a predator, however, the same individuals will join together to stand against threats, a phenomenon that is obvious to anyone who has spent time along the javelinas, the peccaries of the Sonoran Desert. One of the strongest memories from my childhood was watching a group of peccaries treeing (or rather "saguaroing") a bobcat in Disney's *The Living Desert*.

Competition and cooperation go hand and hand in mediating intraspecific social dynamics, because of close and regular interactions between members of the same local population. Can the same be said of interactions between, or more accurately among, species?

As other contributors in this collection have suggested, debates about the relative importance of competition and collaboration underlie a century-old struggle among scholars to shape the very concept of ecological communities. Where numerous species co-evolve, they come to coexist through the combined processes of intraspecific and interspecific interactions. This includes predation and competition, as well as facilitation, commensalism, and mutualism.

When I delve into interactions between different species I know well, the boundary line becomes murkier. My mandate is to focus on fauna, but in my experience with interspecies interactions, that word has a slippery texture. Does it include bacteria and protists, or is it restricted to multicellular mobile species? Even among multicellular lifeforms, we have fungi, the closest relatives to animals.

As a graduate student, I was fortunate to attend a seminar by Ford Doolittle, whose work revealed that the genome of mitochondria was bacterial and bore little resemblance to their host's genome.

Many interspecific interactions in deserts involve bacteria and fungi, especially when the latter combine to form lichens. In the Negev Desert of Israel and Jordan, the soil is heavily covered by lichens, which secrete polysaccharides that bind the soil and sand to form a crust that protects them from heat. These patches reduce absorption of water, increasing runoff, which forms pools in pits dug by desert porcupines. These microhabitats act as oases where wind-dispersed seeds accumulate, growing into small local communities that support other plants, insects, and microorganisms.

This is a classic case of *niche construction,* a rather new idea in evolutionary ecology. This concept helps us identify interactions from which novel microhabitats emerge, although some of these interactions may not be strictly cooperative in the classic sense of the term. When I learned of niche construction, I recognized it as another part of my childhood learning, in which I noticed how animals and plants cooperatively shaped their shared environment.

One remarkable example of niche construction comes from the Negev Desert, where snails eat endolithic lichens. In the process, they disrupt and ingest the rock substrate, weathering down a stony matrix by as much as a metric ton/hectare per year. Combined with snail fecal material, decomposed rock becomes a major agent in soil formation, allowing many other species to move into the rhizosphere, generating more diverse soil invertebrate and microbial communities.

As I learned as a child, humans are the ultimate niche constructors. Well before the invasion by Europeans, indigenous peoples in American deserts were altering landscapes and moving around plants and animals, such as introducing chuckwallas as emergency food sources to islands in the Sea of Cortés. These cultural dispersals allowed the introduced species to occupy new niches that altered the plant and arthropod communities of these desert islands.

All such phenomena fit within the *meandering stream*—a notion noted elsewhere in this collection. We, as land dwellers, are part of the flow of that desert stream.

AT THE DESERT'S EDGE

BENJAMIN T. WILDER

I was born and raised at the base of Mt. Wasson (a.k.a. Wasson Peak) in the Tucson Mountains, where the desert outside my parents' house beckoned me to explore from an early age. I made fort walls of saguaro ribs ringed by moats of prickly pear cactus. Packrat middens outside the garage were sprinkled with childhood toys, Lego men, and Playmobil parts. A graveyard of basketballs held victims of spines from shots gone awry. The desert was a constant backdrop, merging with my psyche.

As my interests gravitated toward natural history and better understanding the desert that encircled my childhood, I began to hear about vast desert regions to the south. Statements blurred into questions that begged for clarity.

More than two-thirds of the Sonoran Desert is in Mexico? The majority of the desert flora is evolved from tropical environments? The desert is a new thing, only appearing on the landscape several thousand years ago? Our desert has its own sea?

As I progressed in my studies and readings, it gradually set in that the saguaro- and palo verde–dominated desert world I grew up knowing was just a fraction of this biome. I clearly recall as an undergraduate the first time I saw Forrest Shreve's defining map: it plainly showed Tucson on the periphery, tucked into the northeast corner of the full expanse of this semi-arid biome.

Since this realization, I have been drawn to decipher how this desert originated and discover its many ways of being. And yet, I continue to ponder Shreve's words associated with that iconic map: "As a geographical entity the Sonoran Desert may be most simply described as the region immediately surrounding the head of the Gulf of California" (Shreve and Wiggins 1962).

I first saw the desert meet the sea where the massive sloping bajada of the east side of Isla Tiburón grades into the Canal del Infiernillo, a water-filled valley that separates Mexico's largest island. My mind was afire, and my heart was immediately rooted to where worlds come together.

Three years later, standing on the summit of Isla Tiburón in a quest to document its unknown flora, the full extent of the Gulf's Midriff Islands lay out in front of me (Felger, Wilder, and Romero-Morales 2012). The Baja California peninsula was to the west and Sonora on the east, with a chain of islands like an artisan belt linking the two. Yet, just as the picture began to come into focus, mysteries appeared. Questions beget questions.

Hiking up in elevation in the desert is walking back in time. The Sky Island Mountains that dot southeast Arizona and northeast Sonora hold remnants of ancient forests that not too distantly occupied the lowlands where the desert is today, forced up in elevation as the climate warmed.

Going up the nine-hundred-meter peak of Isla Tiburón is stepping into the unknown. When we reached the upper ridge, an enigmatic plant, one of the crucifixion thorns, *Canotia holacantha*, was there to greet us, hundreds of kilometers farther south than previously reported. Its presence instantly signaled that this island had an unexpected past. What was this temperate species doing at the center of the desert?

Ping-ponging across the Mogollon Rim of central Arizona, the northern edge of the desert, I found myself stopping in between populations of *Canotia*, here a dominant member of the landscape. Like a Plinko chip dropping through its spiny stems, I was there to collect its DNA to tell me the secrets of its past. Samples from throughout the species range and from its narrowly restricted sister species in the Chihuahuan Desert revealed high degrees of genetic diversity in the south, with evidence of recent expansion into the north, the opposite of what I expected.

It seems that, like me, this arid-adapted desert denizen had tracked the desert's edge—me out of a yearning to better know my homeland, the crucifixion thorn as the climate warmed and other arid taxa expanded north and upslope.

The desert has come and gone throughout the past 2.4 million years of the Pleistocene, stretching its legs during the relatively brief interglacials, then retreating to pockets with stable aridity. Fossil packrat middens, time capsules of desert vegetation curated by those fastidious home makers, have revealed the individualistic nature of species in response to climate change.

Each species, and, as more data are signaling, genetically coherent population, shifts its range in its own way. Saguaros arrived before ironwoods, followed by palo verdes. The community we refer to today as the Sonoran Desert is a new thing, distinct from what was here before or what will be in the future.

How will the desert continue to shift and change? What does a warming climate with amplified extreme events mean to life in the desert? Doomsday scenarios loom, yet if any biota knows how to deal with a hot and variable environment, it is that of the desert. Certain traits will be favored over others, with a predilection for rapid adaptation.

Pick a piece of land, however large or small, to allow you to track the changes. Select a species or two. Map them, count them, draw them. Then do it again the next year, and again.

Teach your children to do the same. We—you and I, the saguaros, the doves, and the bats—are on this unknown trajectory together. The saguaros have seen it before, but at this pace? They may know a trick or two, which we can learn from if we know how to listen.

Searching for how the desert came to be and where it is going is like hunting for the snark. It is a magical path that takes one to the center of the desert, to its outer limits, and back again. I find myself chasing these secrets, staring into the edge.

References

Felger, Richard Stephen, Benjamin T. Wilder, and Humberto Romero-Morales. 2012. *Plant Life of a Desert Archipelago*. Tucson: University of Arizona Press.

Shreve, Forrest, and Ira Wiggins. 1962. *The Vegetation and Flora of the Sonoran Desert*. Palo Alto, CA: Stanford University Press.

DESERT
CONTEMPLATIVES

THE INSURMOUNTABLE DARKNESS OF LOVE

DOUGLAS CHRISTIE

The cave-dark we were born in calls us back.
—KATHLEEN JAMIE

The approach is awkward, difficult. I am crouched over, moving slowly, tentatively into the deepening darkness. Nothing but solid rock all around me. Ahead of me, unknown depth.

The Inner Mountain: this is how the place has been known since at least the late fourth century, when St. Antony first arrived here—a remote place of stark beauty and profound silence at the far edge of the eastern Sahara Desert. Here, according to the stories told of the early Christian monks, Antony lived, in almost total solitude, for the greater part of his life, hidden away inside the mountain. And now, for reasons I cannot easily describe, I make my own descent into the heart of this mountain.

It feels impossibly long ago—the late 1970s—that I first encountered the stories of the early Christian monks and the desert places where they lived. Helen Waddell was my first guide to that world, a worn copy of her classic *Desert Fathers* plucked off the shelf at Logos Books in Santa Cruz, California. In those pages I first came upon the names Mt. Nitria, Cellia, Skete, the Inner Mountain: wild, strange places in the Egyptian desert far beyond my capacity to imagine. But also irresistible.

There, too, I caught my first glimpse of the figures who had long ago withdrawn into the desert silence, as well as their spare, often uncompromising wisdom teachings. The call to enter solitude, for example, is captured in Abba Moses's emblematic saying: "Sit in your cell and your cell will teach you everything." How many of the early monks took this saying to heart? Antony certainly: the image of the monk alone in his cave, struggling with demons, reverberated endlessly in the Christian imagination.

But there was also the deep conviction that the work of the cell is always undertaken within the context of community. "Our life and death is with our neighbor," declared Abba Antony. "If we gain our brother [or sister], we have gained God, but if we scandalize our brother [or sister], we have sinned against Christ" (Curley 2017). Spoken out of the depths of his own long sojourn in solitude.

The cell. The neighbor. Solitude. Community. A fundamental paradox of desert monastic practice. Solitude, silence, and darkness as elemental, the very ground of this practice. But also, emerging from that ground: simple, unwavering attention to one's neighbor. Love born of solitude, silence, and darkness.

The later Christian mystical tradition would make much of this intuition, locating the heart of love's transformative work in the darkness of the abyss. John of Ruusbroec (1900), in his *Spiritual Espousals*, describes the ultimate end of the spiritual journey as "the dark silence in which all the loving are lost." Marguerite Porete (1981) cherishes "the bottomless depths," "the nakedness," and the "nothingness" into which love leads the soul. John of the Cross (1900), in his *Dark Night of the Soul*, exults: "O night more lovely than the dawn! / O night that has united / the Lover with His beloved / Transforming the beloved in her Lover." And Hadewijch of Brabant speaks of the "deepest abyss" as "love's most beautiful form" (Mommaers and Daróczi 2014).

There is no denying the allure of this vision of love: the dark silence, the night more lovely than the dawn, the endless reach and depth of the space in which love flourishes. Who would not want to enter such a space? Many did and continue to do so. Still, the initial allure is deceptive. It gives way eventually to something more difficult and painful and bewildering.

John of the Cross (1900) reports that on that momentous night, his beloved "wounded [his] neck." For Ruusbroec, there is the mournful, aching reality of loss: in the dark silence, he says "all the loving are lost." Marguerite Porete (1981) testifies that souls embarked on the spiritual path must continuously struggle with the "Love by whom alone they are exiled, anni-hilated and forgotten." And Hadewijch claims that "to founder unceasingly in heat and cold, / In the deep, insurmountable darkness of love, / This outdoes the torments of hell" (Mommaers and Daróczi 2014).

The cave is deeper than I imagined. Much deeper. But I keep moving, a thin film of perspiration forming on my neck and arms. Is it the temperature? Or my nerves? I am not sure. After a few minutes, I reach what I take to be the heart of the cave. I notice that the space has opened up to form a kind of bowl. Before me stands a small simple altar on which several candles are burning. Dark red carpets line the floor. The faint smell of melted wax. Light flickering on the rock. Silence.

I sit and lean my back against the cold hard stone. My mind is blank. But I am feeling so many things. Uneasiness at having descended so far down into this dark, empty place. Also a sense of absurdity: what am I even doing here? But what I feel most acutely is a deep, aching loss. Loneliness. Sadness. The image of my mother lying in that hospital bed, struggling with her final rasp-ing breaths, rises before me in the darkness. She is gone. So is my marriage; it has become a hollowed-out place, bereft of intimacy and joy. I know the end is not far off now.

Not long before I departed for Egypt, I read these words of Micheline Aharion Marcom (2004): "The man who has no mother's form to form him is a sad man, unanchored man, vile and demoniac." Too strong? I don't think so. I have become that man and carry the weight of my sadness into the desert.

Still, it feels good to be here, tucked inside the mountain, held in the warm stillness of this space. Just be here, I think. I close my eyes, descending farther into the darkness and silent stillness of the place. I wait.

After a few moments, I open my eyes and slowly scan the walls of the cave. I notice a niche in the rock stuffed with tiny pieces of paper. I pull one out and unfold it: words scrawled in Arabic. Another: the same. And yet another. Dozens of little pieces of paper crammed into this cleft in the rock. Later, I ask my host about this, and he confirms my hunch: they are prayers left for the saint. Prayers expressing who knows how much hidden grief and longing, still unrealized desires and hopes, written on scraps of paper, stuffed into a niche in a cave in the heart of the Egyptian desert. Amazing.

I consider all those souls who have journeyed to this place before me, and who felt moved to unburden themselves in the presence of the saint. Who allowed themselves to become vulnerable in this way. To hope. Who clearly sensed that the one who disappeared into this mountain all those years ago was alive and present to them and held their lives and their well-being close. Who felt, as I do now, that it makes a difference to come here, to enter the darkness, to allow yourself to become vulnerable, to open yourself to the immense silence.

The insurmountable darkness of love.

What is this love born of and nurtured in darkness? Why does love require darkness, silence, and space to grow and deepen? And what do we make of the acute sense of wounding, loss, and exile that haunts our experiences of love and seems both inevitable and necessary to the work of love?

I am aware of how difficult these questions are. I take comfort in knowing that others, including all those desert travelers who have come here before me, have also found them to be immensely difficult. Verging on the impossible. But also unavoidable, necessary, fundamental. So, too, for me.

I think (and do not think) of these things as I slowly crawl back out of the mountain. At the mouth of the cave, I pull myself upright and stand blinking for a few moments in the harsh glare of the desert sun. I scan the vast horizon. Then I make my way slowly down the rocky path and back to the monastery. I reach the gate of the enclosure, cross the courtyard, enter my little cell, and fall fast asleep.

References

Curley, Abba Anthony. 2017. *The Thirty Eight Sayings of Saint Antony the Great: Sayings of the Desert Fathers*. Vol. 1. Scotts Valley, CA: CreateSpace.

Marcom, Micheline Aharonian. 2004. *The Daydreaming Boy*. New York: Riverhead Books.

Mommaers, P., and A. Daróczi, eds. 2014. *Hadewijch: The Complete Letters*. Leuven: Peeters.

Porete, Marguerite. 1981. *A Mirror for Simple Souls: The Mystical Work of Marguerite Porete*. New York: Crossroad.

Ruusbroec, John of. 1900. *The Spiritual Espousals*. London: Farber and Farber.

Saint John of the Cross. 1900. *Dark Night of the Soul*. London: Burns and Oates.

FALLING IN LOVE

TESSA BIELECKI

I first fell in love with the desert in 1967, when I moved to Sedona, Arizona, to join the Spiritual Life Institute. I had grown up in lush green New England, yet I loved everything about the desert: the heat and aridity, the stark landscape and sparse vegetation, the clear air and bright skies, the spaciousness and the silence.

I learned how to garden in dry soil, to watch the habits and habitats of shy desert animals and cheeky birds, to wait through long droughts and then revere the power of lightning, thunder, and flash floods through the dry, snaking arroyos. I gathered rocks, bones bleached white in the glaring sun, cactus "skeletons," dried seedpods, and grasses.

I learned the names of the wild plants because they were my friends and companions: brittlebush, sacred datura, globemallow. I discovered where they lived and when they might appear, but they were always surprising me.

I was enthralled by the saguaro, which I had first seen in movie westerns and the cowboy TV shows that fueled my childhood imagination in the 1950s. The saguaro was the logo of the Spiritual Life Institute, coupled with a passage from the Hebrew prophet Hosea: "I will lead you into the desert, and there I will speak to your heart."

When we lost our Sedona center to land developers in 1983, I was heartbroken. But a new desert found its way into my heart. Soon after we relocated the Spiritual Life Institute to Crestone, Colorado, the monks who moved there first took me to the Great Sand Dunes an hour away. The massive rounded dunes reminded me of the Sahara and seemed as close as I would ever get to the North African desert that has always fascinated me.

I looked at the vast expanse before me and said out loud, "Finding this is worth losing Sedona." As I wandered the dunes over the next thirty years with friends and fellow monks, with students from the classes I taught at Colorado College, and especially by myself, I always looked for a concaved spot where I lost sight of the surrounding mountains and saw only sand and sky.

I left the Spiritual Life Institute in 2005 under tragic and traumatic circumstances—an example of the desert as loss and grief—and created a new nonprofit with my fellow desert rat David Denny. Our Desert Foundation was born the very moment we saw the saguaros rising majestically in the wilderness between Phoenix and Cordes Junction on Arizona Highway 17.

We used the saguaro again for our new logo, with another desert passage, this time from the prophet Isaiah: "The desert and the dry land will be glad; the wilderness will rejoice and blossom." A massive full moon rises behind the saguaro.

Why do I love saguaros? As many indigenous people have declared, they are (like) people. Like us, saguaros are made mostly of water and stand upright with trunks and spines, ribs and flesh. When they die, they leave behind starkly beautiful skeletons—and their "boots," another story for another time.

Saguaros also have personality. Each one is different. On my walks through saguaro lands, I find myself spontaneously greeting these behemoths with affectionate nicknames.

The one I call Friend reaches out her two arms to embrace me. Los Abuelos, the Grandparents, have many arms in their old age to hug their many grandchildren. The Sentinels, younger and therefore armless, stand five abreast in a remarkably straight line, keeping watch. The one-eyed Cyclops looks at me grotesquely. The Headless Horseman, despite his name, is more benign and lets a white-winged dove sit on his "neck," while his multiple arms hold tinier songbirds.

What do I learn from the saguaros? Endurance, adaptability, generosity, a sense of mystery and awe. The longer I look at saguaro cactus, the more I notice how many of them carry multiple beautiful scars. So their greatest lesson for me is the *healing of wounds*.

Fifty years after I first "found" the desert in Sedona, I realized I'd spent almost thirty-five years "exiled" from Arizona. I heard myself saying, "I'd move back to Arizona in a heartbeat if I could." And I realized in a heartbeat: "There's no reason I can't."

I heard Alfred, Lord Tennyson, challenging me through his poem "Ulysses": "Come, my friends. 'Tis not too late to seek a newer world."

I knew that sometimes a newer world means coming full circle and rediscovering an older one. So with only a sleeping bag, a blender, and a card table for a desk, I took off for the Sonoran Desert of northwest Tucson. I checked into a hotel while I searched for an apartment close to Saguaro National Park West, so I could walk among the majestic cacti and be close to the Desert House of Prayer, where I could pray in community again.

Finding the desert was love at first sight in 1967, a deeper love in 2017. It felt like coming home—to myself. I recognized the outer landscape of the desert as a mirror of my inner soulscape. The desert is truly the homeland of my heart. I find it not barren but a perfect embodiment of what my Buddhist friends mean by *sunyata*: infinite spaciousness.

My spiritual path is cultivating a heart as spacious as the desert: wide open to every direction of the compass; wide open to every creature that walks, flies, or crawls through it; wide open to every change in the weather—darkness and light, sun and rain, heat, cold, and wind.

ENCOUNTERING OPENNESS

THOMAS LOWE FLEISCHNER

Far too often, deserts are described by alluding to what they *aren't*, by a shortage of water, a modicum of rain, animals that are rarely seen because they hide out in burrows and await the arrival of darkness, plants that must adhere to the strictest rules of hydro-economy, the biophysical comforts—soil, moisture, nutrients, shade—these plants must endure without.

But a desert *is*. It *is* a landscape of invitation and accessibility, where one can walk in any direction without thrashing through branches. It *is* a place where birds perch in the open, at heights humans can easily see. We must carry weighty water and wear a broad-brimmed hat, yes, but naturalists flock here for very good reasons: An opening of light. Expansiveness and possibility. The ability to place one foot in front of the other and move in any direction. To see new birds perched on new shrubs, in clear view.

I penetrated deeper and deeper into the land of seeming nothing, the land without verticality. Wendell Berry once described the sea as "immensity on the loose"; this open country presented an immensity of stillness. In quickening succession, a series of new romances ensued: Malheur, in the Great Basin; Death Valley; the Channeled Scablands of the Columbia Plateau; and then, my great and lasting loves, the Sonoran Desert and the slickrock country of the Colorado Plateau.

I often encounter such a simple set of stark options in the openness of these deserts: I could walk in any direction I wished; I could see the entire plant community, since I was as close to tall as, or taller than, the largest organisms; I could sit and feel the sun on my face.

These shocking simplicities presented the *invitation* of a lifetime, and I accepted. These simplicities encouraged me, ultimately, to consider complexity, with freshly honed perception.

Each of these landscapes with its own seductive charms, its own textures and tastes. The unpredictable scent of sagebrush, slightly dampened by overnight chill. The remarkably smooth walls of Wingate and Navajo sandstone rising above desert streams in which I walk.

White-throated swifts vaulting out of alcoves; ravens croaking high above canyons; the rasping call of a cactus wren, from dense cholla thickets; canyon tree frogs clustered above slickrock pools; toad songs echoing a half mile along Grand Gulch.

Camping with my wife and son, just turned two, in the even coppery sand next to a canyon alcove and finding pot sherds, left by another family a millennium earlier. Landing on the remote island in the Gulf of California with an elder who sang the island's songs on the cobble beach, then walking up the central arroyo—new plants, plants that live only here, giant lizards, this island with its own language.

A friend once mentioned that when he was preparing to move to Arizona from New England that his expectation was of "five thousand square miles of kitty litter." But what I first encountered was the sensuality of these places. Only later did I learn biogeographic descriptors and field marks: bajada, alluvial fan, soil crust, terrace, alcove; Arizona upland and Central Gulf Coast subdivisions; slickrock, desert varnish, and desert pavement.

I began to learn about *time* in all new ways. Sandstone walls built particle by particle and then eroded in the same way. Sitting in silent solitude for two days and nights, how very little "happens"—perhaps a grain or two of sand is plucked away; a raven flaps in, perches, and is gone. And deep time of assemblages moving more or less in sync.

I was astonished to learn that the Sonoran Desert is one of the world's newest kinds of places, just a few thousand years in existence. And yet its ironwood trees and cardón can live as long as conifers in the ancient forests of the Pacific Northwest.

The desert can lull us into pleasant lethargy and can slam us into alertness. After two weeks' immersion in sandstone canyons, lounging by the rarity of a desert pool, ringed by skin-smooth slickrock, like cats in comfort, stretching our paws in the warmth. Then, during the night, rain started raking our camp, soaking gear.

At first light, temperatures plunged, and the rain quickly turned to snow. Whereas a half day earlier we had been seeking shade, some of us now found ourselves with soaked gear, wet shoes and sleeping bags, standing in snow, and with an urgent need to *move*, to get *out*. Yet the canyon we would need to follow for ten miles required numerous crossings of a small stream channel—a channel that had been transformed overnight into a torrent, knee deep, snow cold, and opaque with sediment. The previous afternoon, it had been in the eighties; by tonight, air temperature would sink to single digits.

The desert cannot be taken for granted.

But walk out this morning, golden light haloing the saguaros, the ratcheting raspy song of cactus wrens, and the slurred whistles of thrashers. Or inhale the scent of dawn-damp sagebrush on a terrace below an alcove of smooth, coppery sandstone, where humans have sat for more than a millennium. Watch ice crystals sparkle colors in winter light of the Great Basin.

We love this, all this—not for what it isn't but for what it *is*. And for what it enables in us: a sense of open possibility, of capacity to wander and wonder in almost any direction, of our enhanced drive to *explore* this world. We give thanks for this moment, in this precious desert.

A HOOSIER'S DESERT

FATHER DAVID DENNY

I grew up on a verdant flat earth of hardwoods, redbuds, trillium, limestone caves, muddy lakes, humid summers, incandescent autumns, gray winters, and slushy springs. My parents took my brother and me to state parks named Spring Mill, Turkey Run, and McCormick's Creek. But outside these sanctuaries, it was hard to imagine the land before agriculture. My hometown of Kokomo, Indiana, was surrounded by fields of sorghum, corn, and soybeans.

Around the time Neil Armstrong took his "small step" onto the moon, we moved to Arizona. I was sixteen. One of my earliest Arizona memories finds me lying in an inner tube, floating down the Salt River, my back side chilled, my exposed face and torso baking under the summer sun. Steep stone walls loomed overhead, with saguaros sprouting between the canyon wall tops and the cobalt sky.

A year later I gazed down on another desert, the Dasht e Margo (Desert of Death), before my Ariana Afghan Airlines flight descended into Kabul, where I would spend the summer as an exchange student. I was stunned by how much Afghanistan looked like Arizona from the air, and by how wildly their cultures differed once I moved into my host family's home—not better or worse, but with fascinating, bewildering differences.

Afghanistan led me to study Islam and Arabic at the University of Arizona, and three summers after Kabul, I studied Arabic in Tunis. A bus tour took us students south to the Sahara. We rode camels into the wondrous undulations of sand and spent a night at a date-palm oasis. I remember being dazed by the presence of water, but as the sun set, my friend Pete and I felt drawn out into the emptiness of sand, sky, and the swollen molten sunset.

Between the Dasht e Margo and the Sahara, I encountered two other kinds of desert. My college roommate loaned me Thomas Merton's *Seven Storey Mountain*, and there I discovered the *eremos* (desert) of the first Christian hermit monks. I was delighted to discover this Middle Eastern and North African foundation for Christian monasticism and shocked to learn that Christian monks still exist. My friends and I were aware of teachers from India, Tibet, and Southeast Asia arriving in the West to teach meditation, and we had at least heard of Sufism, but I was completely ignorant of the Christian mystical, contemplative tradition.

And then I spent my twentieth birthday in a Buddhist monastery, on a three-week *vipassana* (insight) meditation retreat. For me, the nontheistic experience of impermanence, unsatisfaction, and no-self did not feel peaceful or liberating. It was profoundly *other*. My childhood understanding of ultimate reality personified in an Abrahamic God was, for some very wise and transformed people and their sacred cultures, simply irrelevant.

My experience may have been somewhat enlightening, but it felt like endarkenment, loss, not a wondrous desert of space and freedom but a serious challenge to a loving bedrock God of Moses and Jesus who shares eternal life and love with us. I thirsted for a deeper love and understanding of Christ's glory, as well as a deeper trust in my intuition that ultimate reality is characterized by an I and a Thou.

I never fully returned from Kabul or from that Buddhist retreat. I was changed, and it was impossible to "go back." My unreflecting immersion in American culture and primitive grasp of Abrahamic monotheism *deserted* me.

What to do? I followed a revolutionary yet ancient instinct. I sought radical personal transformation. I needed more than books to prepare me to serve a wondrous sacred world that suffers unending warfare and appalling injustice.

Like men and women of the fourth century, I entered a monastery.

I did not feel a need to escape my culture's demands but was attracted to something more demanding, yet lovely, generative, and freeing: the desert, where I would wrestle with demons and, if lucky, be wounded by an angel. It did not hurt that the monastery was in the chaparral country of Sedona, Arizona.

I thought my monastic adventure would be a brief immersion for a few months before graduate school. It lasted thirty years. And afterward, if anything, my life is even more "deserty" than ever, since I live in an isolated valley where I have more solitude and see more mule deer than people in an average week.

I have never outgrown my fascination with the Sonoran Desert, and I hope to return there to live and die. I love its physical characteristics, its "body," from canyons to cactus wrens and curve-billed thrashers, from saguaros to scorpions. Its ecosystem is ancient, raw, and elegantly intertwined.

And what I love about the inner deserts is that they have taught me by depriving me of my narrow native worldview, introducing me to unimaginable space and beauty. Hollowed out, I learned to be more hospitable to other worldviews and religions. There is space.

Some aspects of Abrahamic monotheism need the tempering, purifying wisdom of the Buddha. He was for me like John the Baptist, preparing the way for a new creation. The violent, tribal dualism that has plagued Western religion benefits from the nondualistic intuition of interbeing more common in Asian spirituality.

In college, I had learned in a desert ecology class that certain species thrive, and communities become healthier when they intermingle, cross-fertilize. I could never have imagined how enlivened I would be by my brushes with other worlds that undermined my flat earth, with the desert world of life bursting from aridity, maybe even from death.

I hope my decades in the desert, my "small steps" toward the heart of the earth and the human heart, encourage my neighbors to take their own steps into the inevitable healing desert, which makes space for the other and gives birth to the fullness of life.

LISTENING TO OUR SIBLING DESERTS

Restoring Indigenous Mindfulness

JACK LOEFFLER

Over the last sixty years of my life, I have worked, hiked, herded sheep, backpacked, river rafted, ridden fence by horseback, performed music for nearby detonations of atomic bombs, manned a fire lookout, meditated, and recorded voices of fellow creatures within their natural habitats throughout the vast span of our four North American deserts and surrounding environs. I've been privileged to conduct recorded interviews with hundreds of Native farmers, herders, medicine men, weavers, foragers, foresters, hunters, lore masters, singers of sacred songs, and other fellow humans who have sustained themselves from within the presumed "meager resources" of these arid lands.

As I have recorded them, I have often had the feeling that each is speaking of one's desert homeland as a complex landscape that is both intelligent and subject to many moods. No matter whether you call it a community, an ecosystem, or an eco-region, it responds to you as a greater living entity in which you intuitively take part, as within the life dance of mutual reciprocity.

For years, this has seemed a somewhat preposterous notion to many educated within the prevailing cultural norm. Yet, I found some recognition for this worldview in the writings of the great naturist/anarchist philosopher Pyotr Kropotkin, and in conversations with my pal Ed Abbey and several other naturalists, contemplatives, and desert rats I have known. But it was not until Fritzof Capra spoke to me of the scientific collaborations of Maturana and Varela that I saw the natural sciences embracing such a notion: "Living systems are cognitive systems, and living as a process is a process of cognition. This statement is lawful for all organisms, with or without a nervous system."

So wrote Humberto Maturana and Francisco Varela, the brilliant Chilean biologists who forwarded the theory of autopoiesis, which addresses living systems as being capable of self-regeneration and self-maintenance. Their theory strongly suggests that life and cognition are two aspects of the same phenomenon, one in which each cell is a living cognitive system, itself part of a greater system of organisms composing the biotic communities that span the biosphere that encompasses our planet Earth.

Life emerged as a continuum on Earth nearly four billion years ago according to the tome of science. Indeed, all life is thought by some to have descended from a single cell that blinked into existence possibly near a hydrothermal vent in an ancient sea.

This was our last universal common ancestor (LUCA). LUCA spawned life and cognition and thus transformed our planet Earth into a living cognitive system, spinning in space, through time, around our sun, in a remote neighborhood of our galaxy, itself one of an estimated two trillion galaxies separated by space, all of which compose our known universe. Just think—from micro to macro in the blink of an eye.

Consider this—life and cognition gradually evolved on Earth over the millennia into levels of consciousness as experienced by humans and other species whose individual organisms comprise trillions of living cognitive cells glommed together, genetically programmed to result in folks like you and me, as well as octopuses, dolphins, and members of other species, whose forms of consciousness may seem alien to us but were spawned of the same Earth warmed by the same sun, nurtured by the flow of nature. This may be difficult to grasp intellectually but not intuitively. And intuition is part of cognition, part of consciousness.

I like to think of ecosystems as gardens of cognition. Desert ecosystems somehow seem easier to perceive than, say, jungle ecosystems. No matter where one is in a jungle, the jungle is up close and in your face. But deserts have a lot of open space, and their inhabitants—floral, faunal, and otherwise—live in less crowded conditions. Those of us ignominiously known as "desert rats" are lured to deserts just as pollinators are lured to blossoms, perchance that our consciousness may itself blossom to drop a seed here and there to possibly bloom into a mighty notion, or simply to satisfy the deep urge to linger in life, to ruminate within the larger garden of cognition.

The patterns of North American deserts can be regarded as mosaics of ecosystems, each distinct yet collectively characterized by aridity. Four different deserts lie within the physiographic province known as the basin and range, wherein mountain ranges ripple across seas of desert soils. Each desert is wildly beautiful and rampant in its moods. Our deserts define themselves according to their own bio-cognitive criteria.

Take the Sonoran Desert, regarded by many as the most luxuriant desert in North America. It is characterized in part by great columnar cacti, including both saguaro and organ pipe. Birds abound, and there are bees and other insects galore. Reptiles may lurk in every shadow, while dozens of species of mammals thrive, as life feeds on life in a dance of mutual participation that defines this desert ecosystem.

Indeed, the Sonoran Desert is a *commons*, a natural habitat from which every organism sips its sustenance, an environment that evolved in response to long-term weather patterns, which shaped and reshaped the nature of the biotic community contained within a gradually ever-shifting geophysical cradle that provides common homeland to every living creature. It is one of many commons that make up the biosphere—the land, the water, the air—of our living planet, Earth. For me, the Sonoran Desert is also a metaphor for the commons of human consciousness.

Humans have passed through this commons since before the end of the last ice age, when piñon, juniper, and small oak trees still dotted the landscape before retreating uphill to seek cooler homelands. As the Pleistocene warmed into the Holocene, human cultures evolved within the context of the changing habitat, establishing a sense of deep indigeneity, always realigning human consciousness with the ever-changing bio-cognitive garden now known as the Sonoran Desert. These humans integrated themselves into the Sonoran biotic community, fully recognizing their kindredness intuitively as well as intellectually. Many of their descendants still do.

My late friend Danny Lopez was a Tohono O'odham elder, whose ancestors' cultural perspectives were shaped by the flow of nature through the Sonoran Desert. Early one morning twenty years ago, Danny and I met to have a conversation. We sat down in the shade of a palo verde tree, I turned on my recorder, and Danny spoke to me of his cultural perspective:

> The land was always considered to be something special. They even used to say that the land was a person, and the plants were respected because certain plants give us medicine. As I sit here, I'm looking at all the creosote in front of me because creosote is one of the plants that we call a medicinal plant. The Earth helps us, so we respect the Earth. Certain plants were our food, like the saguaro. We eat the saguaro fruit, the cholla buds, prickly pear, the wild spinach, those little buds called Papago lily. The plants help us so we have a lot of respect for certain plants. Before you first eat the seeds of the prickly pear fruit, you talk to it, you pray to it—especially the saguaro fruit. We say the saguaro is a person. We take a little of the saguaro fruit, and we place it over our heart, and we pray.
>
> We have to take care of our mind, our body. We pray in the morning. We can pray any time. I do that whether I'm up on that mountain or out here. You can pray any place and talk to whatever you believe in. Practice your faith, whatever it is, and live it, because that's what the old people did. They lived it, they shared, they gave, they made other people happy. Because if we don't, we're going to become more violent. Prayer is there for a purpose, whether it's the O'odham prayers or a song.

Danny Lopez talked to me in this way for a long time. After he finished, we were silent for a while, both of us listening to the songs of our fellow creatures, the morning bio-phony of the Sonoran Desert. I realized then that Danny had revealed to me the state of indigenous mindfulness, which traditional people who are native to their homeland cultivate. Their reverence for the natural world is honed by knowing that humans are part of the natural world, that everything is integrated, everything is sacred. As Danny and I sat there quietly looking out over the Sonoran Desert, I once again understood that Danny and I were part of the wildlife released into consciousness by the flow of nature. Danny was reminding me that we must restore indigenous mindfulness within the commons of human consciousness, lest we so cloud our minds with presumed human needs, will to power, misplaced fealty, and hubris that we lose our way through life.

A second O'odham master of desert lore, Camillus Lopez, once said to me: "If you look into the mirror of Nature and cannot see yourself in it, then you are too far away."

DESERT AS ATZLÁN AND DIVIDED TURF

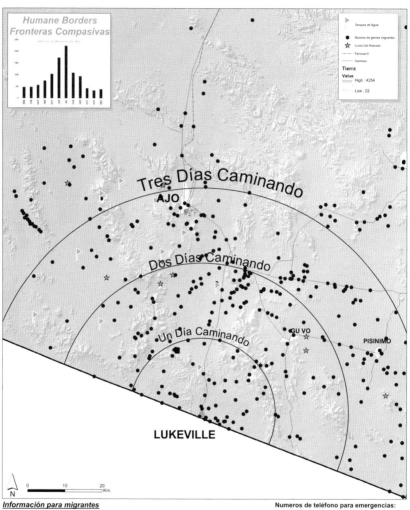

Humane Borders
Fronteras Compasivas

Tres Días Caminando

AJO

Dos Días Caminando

Un Día Caminando

GU VO

PISINIMO

LUKEVILLE

Tanques de Agua
Muertos de gentes migrantes
Luces Del Rescate
Ferrocarril
Caminos

Tierra
Value
High : 4254
Low : 22

0   10   20
━━━━━━━━━━ Km.
N

Información para migrantes

Pasar la frontera caminando por el desierto es peligroso y puede terminar en la muerte.

Si decides pasar la frontera a pie, prepárate bien.
- Ve con gente que conoce y en la que confías.
- No cruces el desierto entre mayo y agosto ya que las temperaturas son mu altas.
- Trae bastante agua y comida.
- Conoce bien la ruta y la distancia antes de comenzar.
- Busca los tanques de agua en el desierto señalados con banderas azules.
- Puede hacer mucho calor en el día y frío en el noche.
- Use ropa adecuada y botas o zapatos tenis.
- Lleva tus documentos importantes: tu identificación y los números de teléfono de tus parientes o amigos con quien puedes comunicarte en caso de emergencia.

Numeros de teléfono para emergencias:
Patrulla Fronteriza: (877) 872-7435
Policía: 911
Consulado Mexicano: (520) 882-5595
Grupo Beta de Sasabe: (01152) 637-374-8076

¡NO VAYA UD!
¡NO HAY SUFICIENTE AGUA!
¡NO VALE LA PENA!

CLEARLY MARKED GHOSTS

FRANCISCO CANTÚ

In the fall of 2015, I asked undergraduate students enrolled in my honors
English course at the University of Arizona to spend a semester thinking
about maps and the stories they tell. Their first assignment was to choose
a map and analyze its rhetoric: who is the map's author, who is the map's
intended audience, what is the mapmaker's purpose?

One of my students, a soft-spoken forty-year-old undergraduate from
England named Rupert, was drawn to a map published by the nonprofit
humanitarian aid group Humane Borders. The map he chose depicts the
southwestern corner of Arizona and plots the deaths of undocumented
migrants who lost their lives crossing the border in this remote tract of the
Sonoran Desert from 2000 through 2013. According to Humane Borders, the
map was designed for distribution south of the U.S. border at shelters and
other waypoints along the migrant trail.

The map is peppered with hundreds of red dots, each representing the
GPS coordinates where the recovery of a dead body was reported by the U.S.
Border Patrol, the Yuma County Sheriff, or the medical examiners of Pima
and Maricopa Counties. Included are visual overlays indicating the number

of days required to walk corresponding distances on the map, a bar graph representing the average number of deaths per month, and icons signaling the location of water tanks and rescue beacons.

In Rupert's rhetorical analysis of the map, he describes it as a "warning poster . . . designed more to scare, reminding people what has to be faced." He writes that "by presenting the deaths marked in red so prominently, along with the other data . . . this poster reads like a 'keep out' sign not dissimilar to the ones found on the boundaries of private property or on military land where unexploded ordnances may exist or where land mines are deliberately present." At the bottom of the map bolded text cautions potential crossers in all caps: DON'T GO! THERE'S NO WATER! IT'S NOT WORTH IT! Rupert also recognized that the map serves as more than a simple tool for dissuasion. "The map's small red circles," he writes, "mark points of departure from this life, acknowledging people's previous existence, like memories remembered by family and friends. Usually with no form of identification, no passport, no driving license, these people are like ghosts to the authorities in this life, and the next."

Rupert was one of those rare students who would frequently visit me during weekly office hours to discuss writing, share drafts of in-progress essays, and ask for detailed feedback for improving his work, even after it had already been turned in and graded. When Rupert came in to discuss his analysis of the Humane Borders map, I acknowledged that he had chosen a map that broached a difficult and weighty subject. I struggled to find language that could acknowledge the dissociative nature of the map and recognize, at the same time, the reality of the plotted deaths, the individual and cumulative weight of each red dot.

Since Rupert was more than ten years my senior, I was careful not to speak to him in any way that might suggest I saw myself as more experienced or knowledgeable. Perhaps for this reason, as we sat in my office discussing the map's two-dimensional abstraction and reproduction of human death, I declined to tell Rupert that I had spent years mapping this same terrain by hand, that in traversing its landscape I had walked and driven past countless points of departure with little awareness of the lives that had blinked out there, or that I had once looked on a dead body on the desert floor, that I could likely point to one of the map's red dots and call to mind the face of the man whose death it signified.

After graduating from the Border Patrol academy at twenty-three years old, I was sent to my duty station in southwestern Arizona and assigned to a field training unit alongside my academy classmates and other recently arrived trainees. Our first weeks at the station were wholly dedicated to area orientation, and my first days with a badge and a gun were spent crammed into the back of lumbering patrol vehicles with my fellow trainees, furiously scribbling notes and sketching maps in a small notebook I carried with me in the cargo pocket of my rough duty pants. As we drove across uneven dirt roads, I filled pages with sloppy lines and quivering handwriting, glancing out the window and repeating place names as I scrawled them in my notebook: there is Diaz Peak; there is Black Mountain; here is Cameron's Tank.

Among the most important information pressed on us in those first weeks on the job were the names of prominent topographical features and human-made landmarks. We were prodded to study from all angles and directions the jagged ridge lines of desert mountain ranges, memorizing the myriad peaks and passes and holding in our minds the foot trails that crossed over them and snaked around their edges. We were made to memorize highway mile markers and corresponding side roads and were quizzed as to which pullouts were favored by drug smugglers and migrants lying in wait for their load vehicles. We were encouraged to see the landscape as crossers might, to look toward the horizon and discern a path of least resistance or a path of greatest obscurity, to recognize places of concealment and waypoints offering shade or a vantage point for surveying terrain, to identify prominent features walkers might use to guide off while making their way through otherwise barren and indistinct stretches of desert.

As we traversed our station's area of operations, the field training officers in charge of orienting us relayed oral histories of the landscape, stories rooted in enforcement, pursuit, and death, often recounted with callous detachment—here is where I was almost run over by smugglers; here is where I ran over a drunk Indian asleep on the road; here are the burned-out cars we lit on fire in the good old days; there is the water tower where agents on horseback captured one hundred walkers; down there is where a group of migrants in torn clothing stumbled out of a canyon after being attacked by a jaguar; here is where an agent crashed into a cow and lost his life in the darkness of early morning. Other times, senior agents would pass along strange and storied place names with little context, pointing toward locations known as the spooky forest, the trail of tears, purgatory, vampire village, Christmas gate, beef stew, dead man's gap. We learned and mapped these places as the agents before us had, with little understanding of the larger narratives that might have surrounded their naming.

At the end of my shift, I would return to the empty house where I lived alone to draw and redraw full-page maps of the terrain I had detailed in my pocket notebook. In a cavernous dining room, I sat delineating highways and dirt roads, fence lines and foot trails, peaks and mountain passes, thinking little of the deaths that had occurred there or those that were yet to come, thinking even less about the weaponized way I was coming to understand the place, about my own role in perpetuating the loss of life that was playing out there. Traversing the landscape by day, I focused instead on naming and navigating space, convincing myself that I was helping to interdict fatigued and dying crossers, rather than grappling with the fact that avoidance of my presence was the very thing pushing them to their deaths.

On August 15, 2010, more than a year after finishing field training and being released for regular patrol, I saw my first dead body in the desert. The body was fresh, lying on a dirt two-track about a hundred yards south of a bend in Indian Route 23, where the road turned to snake through a chain of low hills. When I arrived on the scene, two boys—the dead man's sixteen-year-old nephew and his nineteen-year-old friend, both of them from the same Native village in the Mexican state of Veracruz—stood hovering above the dead man.

What I remember most from that day is the dead man's face, his dark hair and long eyelashes, the way ants traveled in neat lines toward the foam drying

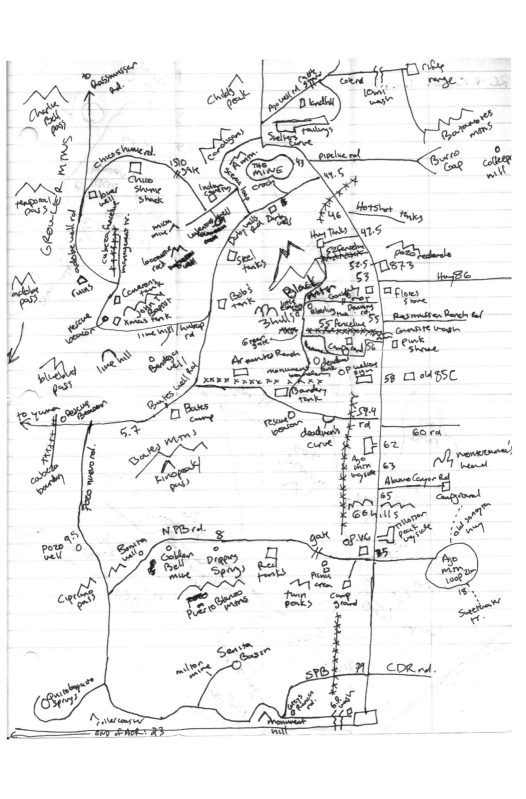

at the corners of his mouth, the way blood pooled in his body to form a long purple line along the length of his torso—a massive horizontal bruise.

I remember, too, the way these boys milled around the dead man's body and looked out in devastation on the desert, as if they had been robbed by some faceless criminal, and how they asked me, naïvely, if they could come with the body to the medical examiner's office, if they could accompany it back to Mexico, if they could bring the dead man back to his family in Veracruz.

The answer, of course, was no, and I can still recall how I was made to explain to the boys, as rain clouds gathered in the distance, that they were in effect under arrest, that shortly they would be taken into custody, separated from the body, and transported to a Border Patrol station to be processed for deportation. Their only recourse to reunite with the body of the dead man, I told them, was to describe their situation to the Mexican Consulate and hope that arrangements could be made for his eventual repatriation to their home state. As I further explained to the boys the vast government bureaucracy that awaited the man's body, I did not realize that I was also articulating out loud, for the first time, the institutional indifference of which I had become a part.

The deadliness that has come to define the borderlands can be traced back, quite plainly, to the 1990s, when Border Patrol chiefs began cracking down on migrant crossings in heavily trafficked urban areas like El Paso and San Diego. Walls were built, budgets ballooned, and scores of new agents were hired to patrol border towns. Everywhere else, it was assumed, the inhospitable desert would do the dirty work of deterring crossers away from the public eye.

Doris Meissner, the commissioner of the Immigration and Naturalization Service from 1993 to 2000, told the *Arizona Republic* that during the adoption of this strategy, which came to be known as "prevention through deterrence," enforcement officials and policymakers believed "that geography would be an ally to us" and that border crossings "would go down to a trickle once people realized what it's like" (Borden 2000). Of course, migrants continued to cross despite the new dangers of the journey, risking their lives in the desert in ways they had never done before. Even as it became obvious that large numbers of people were risking the crossing, resulting in an unprecedented number of deaths being plotted across increasingly remote corners of the desert, the government did not change course.

"I will be absolutely frank with you," Meissner told an interviewer when asked to look back on the policy of deterrence in light of migrant deaths, "the idea of abandoning any kind of strengthened border enforcement because of that consequence was not a point of serious discussion." Meissner's damning admission on behalf of the government—that the sustained loss of hundreds of migrant lives on America's doorstep each year was not significant enough to reevaluate policy—bares the fact that the hundreds of migrants who continue to die here every year are in fact losing their lives by design.

Jason De León, in his book *The Land of Open Graves*, argues that the government views undocumented migrants as people "whose lives have no political or social value" and "whose deaths are of little consequence" (De León 2015). Indeed, deterrence-based enforcement has continued to steer the immigration politics of every administration since that of President Clinton, resulting in an official tally of more than seven thousand migrant deaths along the southern border since the year 2000, a figure that does nothing to account for the thousands more who have been reported disappeared and never found, or those whose bodies have been found but whose names have never been recorded. In 2018, investigative reporter Bob Ortega found that negligent tallying practices by the Border Patrol had failed to account for more than five hundred migrant deaths reported by medical examiners, landowners, and local law enforcement agencies over the last sixteen years— leading to a literal erasure of their lives from official records, a scrubbing of their lives from the landscape.

In Rupert's analysis of the Humane Borders map, he referred to the red dots demarcating migrant deaths as "clearly marked ghosts," small icons that "also indicate the invisible living men and women who were once walking with them at the time of their demise. The people that are still alive and walking."

Reading these words years after leaving my job as a border agent, I was made to think of the boys from Veracruz, and I wondered for the first time how they had borne the news of the man's demise back to his village. I wondered if they still carried him in their hearts, if his loss had ultimately swayed them against attempting another journey, if it compelled them to stay once and for all in their homeland, with all hope of crossing having withered after witnessing a death wholly human made, wholly unnatural—a death that would nevertheless be recorded in the official parlance of the state as having occurred due to simple "exposure" to the unswayable hand of the elements.

In the weeks after I first read Rupert's essay, I had visions of red dots hovering above the terrain where I had worked all those years before. The landscape began to emerge from my mind for what it really was—a place of physical beauty that had been overlaid with death and disappearance. I struggled to connect how the terrain had been shown to me as newly arrived agent with the multitude of deaths that had been fixed on the landscape, in many ways as a direct result of such training writ large. I recalled my hand-drawn maps and thought of how incorrectly they presented the landscape, how wrong it was to represent this desert as anything other than a place marred by the profusion of wrongful and purposeless death.

I wondered, too, about one particular red dot, the one that was, for me, less monstrously abstract than all the others. On a quiet afternoon, I finally sat down to find it, calling up a high-resolution image of the map on the Humane Borders website and zooming in on the terrain to trace the once familiar highways with my finger. Eventually, I found the place where a road turned to snake through low desert hills shaded lightly on the map, a place I had once mapped as little more than a thin line stretching west from the village of Ventana. Placing my finger on the dot, I wondered how the entirety

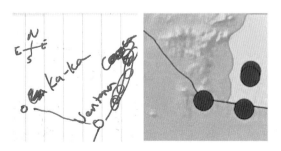

of a man's life had come to be represented by a single point on the map, a red spot identical to hundreds of others flanking it on all sides.

In geographer Denis Wood's book *The Power of Maps*, he asserts that "maps link the territory with what comes with it" (Wood 1992). Thus, in the deadly borderlands of Arizona, perhaps any map that fails to acknowledge the dead—like those that filled my pocket notebook—*should* be seen as problematic or false. But the problem with a map of the dead is that the dead have no names, that their dissimilar lives are represented in the same manner, that each individual is recognized only for their dying, as a "clearly marked ghost" fixed on the landscape.

In beholding a map of dead migrants, the viewer is subtly encouraged to see those who have died crossing the desert in the same way that policymakers and law enforcement agents might see them, the way they are seen by militiamen and human traffickers—each indistinguishable from the next. Indeed, as a uniformed agent standing above the body of a dead man all those years ago, I was somehow never compelled to ask his companions for his name, and even if I had, I would have likely forgotten it quickly and without ceremony.

Even more important than mapping the deaths of border crossers, of course, is preserving the names of those who have died and finding right ways of holding them in our minds, a way that allows us to properly comprehend the spaces in which they have lost their lives. Just as important as their names, but harder to discern, are their stories. A worthwhile map of border deaths would cause us to feel something for each loss of life plotted on it—it would cause us to feel necessarily overwhelmed by the amassing of red dots, by the accumulation of numbers and names, by stories with familiar and comprehensible details.

The importance of names is lost in the warning posters of Humane Borders, but it is not lost on the organization itself. Through a partnership with the Pima County Medical Examiner, Humane Borders maintains a constantly updated and searchable death map online (humaneborders.org), where "viewers may see the exact location where each migrant body has been found, along with other information, such as the name and gender of the deceased (if known and if the family has been notified), date of discovery, and cause of death." Such a tool allows us to interact with the red dots

Case ML 10-01641

Case Report ML 10-01641 Information

Identity: QUECHULPA XICALHUA, ASCENCION, male, Age 29
Reporting Date: 2010-08-16
Corridor: Cowlick
Location: N 32 28.166 W112 16.875
Cause of Death: Exposure
OME Determined COD: HYPERTHERMIA AND DEHYDRATION
County: Pima, Arizona

marking the departed, enables us to hold distinct names in our mind, and provides us with small pieces of information about individual lives—the closing details of stories we might someday seek to understand.

Nearly six years after his death, I drove west from Tucson to see if I could find my way across the desert to the place where the man from Veracruz had laid down to die. I drove along State Route 86 and entered the vast Tohono O'odham Nation, continuing for more than an hour until I reached Indian Route 34. I turned north, passing through long stretches of barren desert on my way to the villages of Hikiwan and Vaya Chin, until I finally reached the junction of Indian Route 23, where I turned to drive toward the village of Ventana.

As I drove west past the village, I began to recognize the low hills in the distance, and I suddenly felt a strange weight, an awareness of the subtle distortions that reverberate in space long after one's death. I drove slowly, nervous that I might not find the exact spot, that I might end up driving for miles wondering if it could have been here or if it might have been there. I began to feel alarmed that I might never stand again in the place where that man's life had ended, the place where his nephew and his companion had stood bewildered as I asked them to explain how the man had met his end.

But then, just before a bend in the road, I saw a dirt two-track splintering south into the creosote flats. I pulled my vehicle onto the dirt shoulder and stepped outside to feel the hot summer wind. In the distance, clouds of clay-colored dust whipped into a tall funnel and then disappeared again at the horizon. As I walked south along the two-track, my memories coalesced on the terrain, and I looked down to find the very patch of dirt where the man had laid on his back all those years ago, with blood pooling in his abdomen and ants crawling across his face. I looked out at the landscape and spoke into the desert air—here is where Ascención Quechulpa Xicalhua ended his life's journey. Here is where his story rests on the earth.

References

Borden, Tessie. 2000. "INS: Border Policy Failed." *Arizona Republic*, August 10.
De León, Jason. 2015. *The Land of Open Graves: Living and Dying on the Migrant Trail*. Oakland: University of California Press.
Wood, Denis, with John Fels. 1992. *The Power of Maps*. New York: Guilford Press.

A WHITE BODY
OUT IN THE DESERT

HOMERO ARIDJIS
TRANSLATED BY GEORGE MCWHIRTHER

For J. M. G. Le Clézio

First we saw a white spot,
away out in the desert. No
doubt, some body sprawled in
the distance, a heat wave off
the sands; a trick of the eye
that will imagine anything, but
doubt its own shadow.

Then we saw the body had an
open door. Some object, no
doubt, dropped out of
imaginary space, a metal bird
with broken wings, some
unserviceable treasure in the
sultry day.

Then, close-up, we discovered
the white spot away out in the
desert was a refrigerator with
an open door.

THE DESERT DARK

RUBÉN MARTÍNEZ

I write about the desert from within the confines of a Cistercian monastery hidden in the undulant forested hills at the edge of the Pacific Ocean in Mendocino County, California, in a region known generally as the Lost Coast. The place lives up to its name. It is remote. The few roads are narrow, serpentine, and canopied by towering redwoods. Driving them in daytime, one darts in and out of pools of deep, almost nocturnal shadow and sudden glaring sunlight. The local population is sparse and very latter-day Northern California: spirit seekers, outsider artists, weed farms on the verge of going corporate, where Mexican immigrants work alongside young white hippies.

I sit at a tiny desk inside my cinderblock cell, looking out onto a meadow of autumnal yellow-gray grass. It has not rained in six months, and it is only a couple of months since the devastating, historic California wildfires of summer 2018. Old-growth trees are plentiful along the Lost Coast, and most of the residences in the monastery are wood-shingle buildings. The place is extremely vulnerable to fire.

I have come here to inhabit a monastic tradition that recedes into (for Americans, anyway) an impossibly remote history. Redwoods Abbey was founded in 1962, but the Cistercian order it belongs to dates back to 1098, and it employs as its spiritual guide the Rule of St. Benedict, written as early as 530 CE. That is a long time to be honing tradition: the liturgy of the hours, simplicity in living quarters, silent meals and *ora et labora*, a life equal parts manual labor and contemplative prayer.

I am writing, then, of two deserts—one material and one transcendent. Christian contemplative tradition casts the desert as its central spiritual metaphor, which turns on the idea of arid lands as empty space (surely upsetting to biologists) relative to the green effusion of riparian areas or the tropics. This was the distinction early Christian mystics made between the densely populated Nile River Valley and the lonely landscapes of Egypt's Eastern Desert. Civilization grew along the river's course; the desert was a place for hermits to hole up in caves and battle demons in emulation of the temptation of Jesus in Judea. Over the centuries and to this day, monks and nuns have retreated to monasteries far from the Sahara, but they imagine an arduous journey as one into the darkness of the desert, hoping to find illumination in the silent land.

This is not the desert I would have written of had our editor, Gary Paul Nabhan, invited me to contribute to an anthology like this a dozen years ago, when I was at work on a book about the deserts of the U.S.-Mexico borderlands. I had not visited the monastery yet, did not even know that it existed. When I thought of the desert—which was all the time, since I'd been living in it for the better part of a decade—I considered the place part of my birthright through my Mexican grandparents, who grew up in the arid lands of northern Mexico.

I also imagined I belonged to it because I am the son and grandson of immigrants from Mexico and El Salvador (the single most important personal and public distinction in my American life—both a point of pride and a collapsed, othered identity). The journey north into the United States from Latin America crosses the desert physically and symbolically. My people wander in the desert, exposed to dangers natural (exposure) and human (Border Patrol), yearning for Canaan. I thought of the desert, then, as a borderland in the material and historical sense. Even more specifically, in the way our cherished late border philosopher Gloria Anzaldúa conceptualized it, the desert for me was an *herida abierta*, an open wound where two nations bleed, violently and politically, erotically and spiritually, into each other.

That desert is still very much on my mind today. The current president of the United States has portrayed an imaginary borderland desert with brutal and crude nativist rhetoric—a fearsome place populated by "bad hombres" and "Middle Easterners." Indeed, there is blood and death in the desert, and not just in the sophomoric symbolic western that Trump conjures. Actual brown bodies with names, hometowns, families, fears, and hopes stumble through the wilderness, fleeing terror in their homelands. They encounter more terror on the road north. They die of exposure (339 deaths so far in 2018, several thousand in the last two decades). They are killed by the Border Patrol (97 fatal officer-involved shootings since 2003). No Border Lives Matter movement registers these bodies in the national consciousness. (Washington is too far away from the desert.)

I bring this desert with me to my other desert, the one in the forest.

I am in the desert in the forest because Douglas Christie, a very tall and generous theologian, friend, and mentor sent me.

I had already become conversant with the elasticity of the desert metaphor by the time I met him: desert as migrant passage, desert as ecologically pure place, desert as John Wayne Americana, desert as spiritual site. I had some sense of the latter, but it was underdeveloped alongside the material, political, and cultural deserts I had narrated and critiqued in my writings.

It took a heart attack to get me there, or at least the one I imagined, the result of a panic attack that took me to the emergency room at St. Francis Memorial Hospital in the wee hours one San Francisco night. I had bolted upright in my hotel room bed, awash in sweat and with stabbing pains in my chest, only to be told by the ER resident doctor with the dissociative bedside manner that my problem was not cardiac but "neurological." (My hypochondriacal mind assumed this meant a brain tumor until I was handed a list of Bay Area psychotherapy clinics.) I walked out into a brilliant autumn morning giddy at having "survived" an encounter with death, an existential black hole I had been orbiting and regularly getting swallowed by since my early twenties. The giddiness did not last long.

My emergency room visit was the culmination of an existential season of artistic frustration and marital tension that in turn had roots in my oldest demons—the darkness of depression and its opposite, mania. The writer could speak only through the manic character, of course, and depression stripped him of his voice. I had swung between these extremes for most of my life, shouting from the roof tops in a righteous prophetic voice one day, and the next, shuttered indoors, mute. To boot, I was a young (though middle-aged) father, facing the array of challenges of anyone starting a family.

I embarked on an intense therapy kick, in a California vein: psychotherapy, psychopharmacology, aromatherapy, hypnotism, mindfulness.

The antidepressants (prescribed for anxiety) made me more anxious.

The aromatherapy made me sneeze.

The hypnotism did absolutely nothing, though I felt so sorry for the hypnotist that I finally (consciously) raised my arm for her on her twenty-fifth suggestion that it was rising of its own volition.

My psychotherapist helped me in his gentle way, but the darkness still pulled at me.

Meditation? It worked. After decades of scoffing at my friends with New Age tendencies, I sat still as often as I could, and occasionally I arrived in the interior desert, drawing a sense of peace I had never felt before. I had worried that by indulging such "soft" practices I would lose my artistic and political edge. But entering the desert of the spirit, I would learn, did not mean a retreat from the world. I had once thought of anything that had a whiff of withdrawal from the world—hermitages, retreats, even mindfulness itself—as an irresponsible escape. I was beginning to understand the opposite: that sometimes withdrawal is a necessary salve for one's wounds—and for the world's.

Not long after the panic attack, I met Douglas—theologian, Californian (every inch a UC Santa Cruz banana slug, down to his perennial flip flops), and, suddenly, my co-teacher in an interdisciplinary (English/theological studies) class we called Into the Desert, the result of a friendly argument that had begun over coffee at our school, Loyola Marymount University. We would both wind up in the desert, or, rather, in different places in the desert. Doug's early research focused on the birth of Christian monastic tradition in the Egyptian desert of Late Antiquity, famously led by the original hermit of Western mystical tradition, St. Antony.

I brought my blend of borderlands deserts, and a radical comparative journey was under way. We would swing from medieval mystic philosopher Meister Eckhart casting the desert as the ultimate metaphor for an ineffable God, to border novelist and poet Cristina Rivera Garza immersing us in the violence of the contemporary desert. Over time, our binary approach gave way to a more integrated vision that would find me dabbling in mindfulness with the students, and Douglas holding forth on racial rifts in America. In one moment, the desert stood for a traumatic absence, and later as a peaceful emptiness beyond our minds so typically cluttered by the everyday. The desert was lack, was fullness, was political or beyond politics, was the canary in the goldmine of climate change, was death, was emergence, was Native land.

My greatest challenge was to find that place where the God of the desert dwells. As I read more Christian monastic history—St. Antony suffering in solitude the assault of demons in his cave—I began to sense that alongside wanting to be a witness to the migrant journey, I was also seeking spirit. Indeed, the migrants themselves had been telling me about it all along. Their journey was a pilgrimage across the desert. Every step in the wilderness was an act of faith.

And so here I am, in the woods, in the desert, in the dark. A dark that can be terrifying but also, on occasion, a passageway to a sense of unity with the all.

On this most recent retreat to the Lost Coast, I have brought with me fresh wounds. The marital tensions had ruptured. I had lost my writerly voice (the desert of writer's block). During these days alongside the Cistercian nuns, who offer me the sweetest, most generous hospitality and profound spiritual accompaniment, the world has crept in as well. There is Wi-Fi here now (a mixed blessing), and the confirmation hearings for soon-to-be supreme court justice Brett Kavanaugh have riveted the country, laying bare the trauma of sexual violence and the silence imposed on it by patriarchy. As for so many Americans, the political became personal in that moment. My life has been filled with survivors; their stories have become intimate. I tried to hold their pain in the desert dark, as the sisters do every day during intercessions, praying for family and friends and for strangers far away.

One morning I arise well before dawn and head out across the meadow toward a grove of redwoods that forms a perimeter around the cloister and the church, where an hour of sitting and walking meditation awaits me. My flashlight is a puny thing in the immense dark of the forest, and sometimes on this walk a primordial paranoia overtakes me. This morning, however, I am sleepy-calm—and of course that is when it happens. I sense movement in the peripheral vision over my left shoulder. I turn to look and what I see, or rather not-see, I can only describe as an *absence*. There is an area of darkness on the meadow about fifty yards from me, about the size of a sedan. I shine my flashlight at it, but there is no reflection—it is like pointing a flashlight into a bottomless well, or at the heavens. I am shocked still and uncomprehending by this. Then the absence abruptly, rapidly, and noiselessly floats across the meadow and into the woods.

I hurry into the redwood grove—which usually gives me the willies—for refuge. In a couple of minutes I am inside the church's comforting predawn semidarkness, where a single candle on a saucer sits on the concrete floor at the center of the nave, and a lamp hangs from the ceiling, casting a cylinder of light over the altar. But the view that dominates here is what is beyond the altar, the clean floor-to-ceiling modernist windows that in daylight look out on the trunk of a massive old-growth redwood but at night are black, save for the faint reflections of our faces looking on the absence where God dwells.

The nuns told me nonchalantly that what I had seen was a bear.

I wrote to an elder of mine, a Catholic writer, and he wrote back that I'd maybe seen the "patron saint of depression"—or a vision of St. Augustine's evil, the absence of good, a black hole in the fabric of the substance of life.

Two darks. Two deserts. One where corruption and violence join to crucify the bodies of the vulnerable; the other where silence is a salve, where no word or image can corrupt what is pure—love, the force that makes the body whole again.

Tonight, hapless and against all odds, hopeful refugees from Honduras are camped out in southern Mexico, in the tropics on their journey into the desert. They are rendered monsters to be contained by the president of my country, and in the hateful echoes of social media that a few days ago focused murderous rage against the Tree of Life Congregation in Pittsburgh. But every step of the way, the refugees are also offered succor and urged on by ordinary Mexicans.

I am in my desert, alongside theirs, writing in the dark.

DESERTS SEEN FROM OTHER PLACES

DESERT EPIPHANY

LARRY STEVENS

JANUARY 1, 2019

I cannot remember a time when I was not obsessively focused on intuiting what living means to other organisms, coping and prospering in this world. At age four, my mother drew my attention to the rough bark of a maple tree, which erupted before my astonished eyes into a flurry of aposematic red and black color as a large but fully camouflaged *Catocala* moth adjusted its hindwings. Child's take home: Not only is all not as it appears, but mystery runs deeper than I can see, or ever imagine.

I spent my youth in the largely antisocial pursuit of eastern North American biota. Turtles were currency in my insect-and-reptile-focused adolescence. My saving graces were my understanding parents and the staff of the Cleveland Museum of Natural History, who let me into the back rooms. There, I spent every hour I could, learning entomology and biology, peering at pinned specimens, trying to interpret and image the environs the collectors hinted at in minute printing on collection labels, and watching ducks land on ice-covered ponds by the art museum.

When I hit the desert half a century ago, it hit back hard, overwhelming and humbling me with its beauty, intricacy, and hard knocks. Running out of water on my first long hike, running free, tirelessly in broken boots, across vast expanses of open desert scrub. But in my initial three years in the desert, I suffered from hydromelancholia, missing the water of my childhood. Until one day, in the back of a pickup roaring across south Phoenix, coming back I think from watching shorebirds at the sewage treatment ponds, my mentor, Roy Johnson, accidentally backed into the sewage, after telling us about a record phalarope he had shot there, that fell into the water, causing him to wade out chest deep in the waste to retrieve the specimen.

Roaring across the Third World backside of "the city where America comes to die," in June, at midday in the blazing hot sun, I got it: full physical acceptance of heat—a desert epiphany. I never looked back from that moment, never questioned the directions this path has taken me.

My stomping ground has mostly been the Grand Canyon, with the study of life there the focus of much of my scientific career. On endless Colorado River research and guiding river trips through those halls of time, I've had the good fortune to have National Park Service collecting permits, to walk with a net ("Annette?" my wife asks), and practice seeing in a landscape where so much has been looked at but so little seen.

Equally important to me, I have had the honor to escort a remarkable array of scientists on those trips—artists, arachnologists, archaeologists, ecologists, geologists, mathematicians, paleontologists, NASA space and deep sea explorers, police psychologists, sound engineers, veterinarians, and zoo keepers. Each has opened my eyes to intimate or extimate dimensions of the world around me, realms to which I was previously oblivious. In Carl Jung's prologue to the translation of the Bardo Thodol, he commented that human consciousness is like an onion, whose layers of perception can be peeled back indefinitely. I would add an inversionary perspective, that the universe around us also expands endlessly, with dimensions, layers of reality, radiating ever outward from our personal consciousness, and from which deep perceptual growth can occur, the "both and more"—breathe both in and out.

Yet, I remain appalled at my ignorance. As a well-intended student and representative of life's supposedly highest form of consciousness, you would suppose that I could figure most everything out here, in the supposedly simplest of biomes. It is dry here, life needs water, but too much as well as too little unweights the fragile balance and trajectory of ecological development, redirects the trajectory and blind path of evolution. But I cannot see through the many skeins and scales of time in my cells that have brought about this contemporary being. I look at the wings of the desert flame skimmer dragonfly and but catch the faintest glimpse of its perilous evolutionary course as its innumerable ancestors flitted through Earth's greatest extinction events. Yet I can scarcely understand how my own portion of life's grand lineage arrived here to see this miracle on the wing.

I am equally appalled at humanity's greed and assumption of primacy over the Earth. Consciousness begets responsibility and compassion, at least for our fellow humans, but in reality, for all life and the well-being of our dear green planet. Our failure to take on that responsibility is nowhere more apparent than in arid regions, where the abuse and unregulated exploitation of groundwater and surface water threatens our very future.

In arid regions, the first principle of governance should and must be to guarantee the sustainability of water supplies. Pope Francis's 2015 encyclical, *Laudato Si*, eloquently and firmly relates environmental with social justice, yet we so arrogantly and pathetically violate that principle every flush: "Me first"; "If I don't use it, someone else will"; all saying, "I just don't care about my child's future."

The desert is not like a woman or a partner in love, with whom delightful entanglements and harrowing personal transcendence are shared. The desert is context, a spatially organized matrix, the Hutchinsonian stage in an evolutionary theater on which countless-since-Miocene generations of adaptation, selection, and blind good luck have sculpted, forged array on array of desert organisms and assemblages, across time and changing landscapes, calling the hand of life time after time, crisis after crisis, in the endless card game of evolutionary grace, a game with brutal rules and from which there is no final result, just an arid-life statement about where we all are now.

Yes, we do not take water, or life, for granted here in the desert: *these are miracles*. Yes, it *takes* guts and brains, luck, and every possible skill to survive long enough to leave one's mark, genetic or intellectual. Yes, I will stay here, remain dumber than a doorknob and more full of it than the Christmas bird, until I drop. And yes, the dry dust I am too soon to become likely will blow northeast, always seeking rain.

LONGING FOR EL MONTE

EXEQUIEL EZCURRA

I was born in northern San Luis, Argentina. That's where the spiny Chaco drylands end and, just some hundred kilometers south, the great Patagonian dry pampas begin, with the tussocky crowns of myriad grasses waving and whispering into the wind.

But where I grew up, you were surrounded by mesquites and creosote bushes and cacti and caranday palms so fierce that if you got stung by the tip of their leaves, it would swell your joints and hurt for weeks. The spiny scrub was known by the locals as *el monte*—the brush—and biogeographers took the name to designate this desert El Desierto del Monte, with capital letters, as if the capitalized name was part of an honorary degree conferred to the thorny wilderness by the pomp of academia.

For me, el monte was simply a beguiling arena for endless adventure and the cosmos for my own exploration of the natural world.

Climate there is staggeringly seasonal. It only rains, when it does, during four months, from December to March, in the South American summer. Huge cumulus clouds start coalescing on the horizon and develop into giant mushroom-like formations of stunning colors. You see them coming from the northwest, rumbling and exploding in thunder and lightning, and suddenly the desert starts smelling like creosote bush and mesquite leaves with the first gust of cool wind.

A few big drops splatter on the parched dusty ground, and a whiff of wet dirt saturates the air in anticipation of the coming storm. And then the entire sky seems to fall on you in a deluge so intense that it makes you wonder if it will ever end, but it stops in a few minutes, and el monte becomes mysteriously silent—a deep, almost religious silence only broken by the short nostalgic chirps of the tinamús.

In summer, once the rains have started, el monte bursts with fruits of all sorts. I used to go out with my childhood buddies to collect sweet mesquite pods called algarroba; the fleshy drupes of *chañar*, a green-stemmed legume tree; the stinkingly sweet, almost fetid coquitos of the palms; and *piquillín*.

Ah, piquillín! It was the joy of my childhood. In the buckthorn family, it produces dense clusters of sugary fruits, like miniature plums, that we used to harvest by placing a canvas under the canopy and beating the shrub with sticks and planks. Then we would gorge on the juicy fruits like they were the last food on earth and happily spend the whole summer in a deliciously oblivious state of osmotic diarrhea.

But no childhood lasts forever, and terrible things, sadly, happen. A military dictatorship forced me to leave my native Argentina lest I join the tragic ranks of so many other *desaparecidos*.

Mexico, a generous country with extraordinarily creative and big-hearted people, opened its doors to me. And so I became Mexican. But the nostalgia for the desert haunted me in the chaos of Mexico City until I visited the Sonoran Desert and saw, with tears in my eyes, similar mesquites, the same creosote bushes, and the same smell of wet dirt when summer thunderstorms arrive.

So I decided that I would be a desert ecologist and study the drylands of Mexico. The rest is simply a résumé, the listings of an academic career. But the true force behind my work was really nostalgia for the desert, the shade of the mesquites, the juicy pulp of the cactus fruits, and the smell of the creosote bushes.

Or, as the rancheros say: *Lo demás, es lo de menos.*

ORIENTED SOUTHWEST

CURT MEINE

My house sits in the shadows of a hundred-foot-high ridge of bare sandstone. It is a south-facing slope, so snow melts more quickly here when the sun shines after a winter squall.

The soil here is sandy, relatively low in nutrients, and drains quickly. But the native grasses that dominate the landscape appreciate it.

When I step outside for a walk, I need to be careful about impaling myself on the spines of cacti.

I live in south-central Wisconsin, fifteen hundred miles from the Sonoran Desert, but I am oriented southwest. In this unglaciated driftless part of the upper Midwest, the sedimentary bedrock lies at the surface in horizontal layers. Squint your eyes when the sun rises, and you can imagine yourself along the San Pedro or Río Grande or the Gila River. Here we call the forms of sandstone bluffs *coulees* and *hollows*; were they a bit larger and drier, we could call them *mesas* and *arroyos*.

On the southwest walls of the main room in my house, I have four large and elegant portraits of native desert grasses. They are the work of Matilda Essig, who has devoted herself to capturing the fine-line forms of the Apache Highlands grasses. When Matilda offered me a can't-say-no bargain on her work, I chose side-oats grama, blue grama, hairy grama, and switchgrass—species with ranges that stretch between and connect the Southwest borderlands and southern Wisconsin. When I look at them, I see way off beyond to the long rays of the sinking Sonoran sun.

And, yes, I can stab myself on either *Opuntia fragilis* (brittle prickly pear) or *Opuntia macrorhiza* (plains prickly pear). I know spots where you can breathe in the brisk conifery air along Lake Superior with prickly pear at your feet.

I live along this continental axis of imagination, defined by its contrasts and gradients, tensions and connections.

By the standards of the flat Midwest, I live in a place of utter irregularity: the elevations in my county go all the way from 715 to 1,593 feet above sea level. Cochise County, Arizona, will take you from 2,419 to 9,763 feet high. In this part of the Midwest, we get thirty-four to thirty-five inches of annual precipitation, distributed along a neat bell curve across the year. The Sonoran Desert may get three to fourteen inches, spiking during the summer monsoon. The sun shines over El Paso 3,760 hours every year. Milwaukee makes do with 2,480 hours. We will go from average daily high and low temperatures of 26 and 11 in January to 82 and 61 in July. In Douglas, Arizona, expect 64/32 and 95/68. Wisconsin is flatter, wetter, cloudier, colder, and greener.

In short, the desert Southwest is rougher, drier, sunnier, warmer, and browner than what occupies me in the cheese-making hinterlands of the Midwest that my friend Gary Nabhan calls "Curdistan."

Across such differences, I find myself always wanting to emphasize continuities, to feel connected across the contrasts. We both had Pleistocene megafauna vulnerable to the business end of Clovis spear points. Wisconsin has its unique concentration (alas, much diminished) of ancient effigy mounds; the Southwest has its cliff dwellings, many dating from the same historical period (a thousand years ago, give or take a couple hundred). Both landscapes hold hard stories of tribal perseverance, determination, and resilience. I like to ponder if native Lake Superior copper ever made it across the continental trade routes to New Mexico's pueblos.

Both landscapes sit along the edge of the bison's historical range. Both still have many bovines, albeit dairy cows in Wisconsin and beef cattle on the semiarid ranges of the borderlands. German immigrants contributed to

Wisconsin's polka tradition and to the *conjunto tejano* of the border country. These days, beef cattle and Midwest dairy cows respond to Spanish voices, on the range and in the milking parlors. Some years ago, neighbors of mine in western Wisconsin created a small nonprofit group, Puentes/Bridges, to foster better understanding between farm owners and operators and immigrant dairy farm workers from Mexico. Every year farmers from Wisconsin go south to visit their employees' home communities, exploring the differences between their cultures and landscapes.

I keep wondering whether these connections are coincidental or more substantial. Here are a handful of particular connections and connectors that I often ponder.

John Wesley Powell came of age on a farm in southeastern Wisconsin, long before he charted the arid canyonlands of the Southwest and documented the region's Native languages and cultures. What mind-set did he bring from better-watered lands to the drier lands beyond the Hundredth Meridian when he proposed that any new development in the West should be organized around watersheds and designed to deal with water scarcity?

Frank Lloyd Wright moved along this Midwest-Southwest axis. His Wisconsin home, Taliesin, is about fifteen miles away from mine as the sandhill crane flies. He built his "natural house . . . native in spirit and the making" of the "yellow sand-limestone" that "lay in strata like outcropping ledges in the facades of the hills" (Wright 2005). Drawn in part perhaps by the comparable geology, Wright began in 1937 to spend his winters at Taliesin West in Scottsdale. I am writing in October. The students in the Taliesin School of Architecture have just made their annual migration to Arizona.

Georgia O'Keeffe was born and grew up in Sun Prairie, Wisconsin, and studied at the Art Institute of Chicago. In the late 1920s she first came to her Faraway and found there her "beautiful, untouched lonely feeling place" (O'Keeffe 1976) at the Ghost Ranch in Abiquiú, New Mexico. Her imagination absorbed desert rock and flower; her vision filled the American imagination in return.

Aldo Leopold grew from midwestern roots and, after schooling in forestry in the East, went to work in the arid Southwest. He married Estella Luna Otero Bergere of Santa Fe. The desert landscape and the cross-cultural marriage contributed to his evolving view of conservation, from a narrowly economic enterprise to a broad cultural aspiration: the "unfolding of a new relationship between people and land" (Leopold 1940).

Leopold was not the only one to be transformed by the contrast. The Midwest's prairies and the Southwest's deserts have both played vital roles in the development of the science of ecology, and the application of that science in conservation. Across the last century, both landscapes served as laboratories for exploring core questions in community ecology. Are plant associations discrete communities of tightly interacting species that change in predictable ways? Or are they loosely organized collections of co-occurring individual species that are subject to unpredictable forces of change? We might cast the tension in that contrast in even broader terms: what is the natural relation between the individual and the community?

Frederic Clements, working in the mixed-grass prairies of Nebraska, was the exemplar of the view that plant communities are akin to superorganisms, following expected stages of development toward a stable "climax" state. Henry Gleason in Illinois and, later, John T. Curtis in Wisconsin looked at midwestern prairies and saw a less structured reality. Individual plant species exhibited their own evolved preferences and tolerances of soil and moisture and other environmental factors, and they constantly changed toward no particular end.

Gleason had an ally in this scientific debate in Forrest Shreve, ecologist at the Carnegie Institution's Desert Laboratory in Tucson (where Clements was also affiliated). Shreve held that it was "nowhere possible to pick out a group of plants which may be thought of as associates without being able to find other localities in which the association has been dissolved" (Shreve 1915). Out of the desert Southwest, too, came revolutionary insights into the role of recurring disturbance—especially fire and drought—in structuring vegetation on the landscape. Such disturbances are not abnormal ecological factors but intrinsic to the character of the place.

It is tempting to map this tension between organismic and individualistic concepts in ecology onto our own human social relations. Are we modest midwesterners, cooperating on our farmsteads and in our small towns and neighborhoods, moderating our extremes to be good neighbors? Or are we ornery desert rats, individualists on the fringe, staying prickly and celebrating our libertarian leanings? I resist the stereotypes and the polarity. I strive for connection along the continuum. We are both and more. We are individuals, dependent on and nested within complex communities. Our lives are, as Aldo Leopold wrote, "conditioned by interwoven cooperations and competitions" (Leopold 1939).

It was Leopold's trail that first carried me into the northern extremities of the Chihuahuan Desert. As an adventuring youngster, I yearned to ground myself in the Gila Wilderness, the nation's first formally designated wilderness area, which Leopold had worked to secure from road development in the early 1920s. I hitchhiked eastbound out of Tucson into what was, for me at least, uncharted territory. Looking south from I-10, I saw for the first time in the distance the mysterious sky islands of the border country. I pledged then and there that I would someday return and enter those alluring blue portals on the far horizon.

My first experience of desert contemplation came on that same trip, along the roadside outside Lordsburg, waiting interminably for a ride on the backroad to Silver City. I sat and stared in silence at the reality before me: roadside gravel and cigarette butts and candy wrappers, grading up and out into scrubby mesquite and ocotillo range, rising up into the higher and distant juniper-piñon green. My naïve desert desire had met its hard and mundane reality, and it stayed there for a few hours.

A ride came, finally, when a kindly latter-day hippie stopped and took me aboard. Across those forty-five miles I was given another desert vision. As we rode up and over the Big Burro Mountains, my driver treated me to a fantastic nonstop oral dissertation on the theme of desert pilgrimage, advancing human consciousness, and the intergalactic dispersion of fungal spores. It was unbelievable.

I had not exhausted my naïveté. I did not realize that I would not really be able to make it into the Gila Wilderness. I would barely have time to walk out of town and just across the boundary line into the Gila National Forest. I did not realize how chilly it could get at six thousand feet elevation on January nights in the desert. But walk I did, out amid the junipers, piñon, and yucca. And camp out I did, with no tent and no pad, shivering in my inadequate sleeping bag on the frigid ground, that first night in the desert that I had envisioned and dreamed of for so long. I was perfectly content to be there, to be connected, and to be cold.

What drives the desire for such connection across landscapes, between the high and dry desert and the mild lowland Midwest? I have to believe it is something much more than just relief from winter's cold (at one end of the axis) or summer's heat (at the other). Every time I trace that transect, in my mind's eye or across actual space, I figure it must have something to do with the craving for contrast, the fascination of diversity, and the need to stretch out. I am no longer a newcomer to the desert. I am a refugee and a returnee. A connector and a conduit. I pitch my tent with stakes sunk on one end into midwestern loam, and on the other into hard-packed southwestern sands.

The weather forecast says that the first frost of the year in Wisconsin is coming two nights from now. I need to go out to my garden and do some late chores. I do believe that, with my sixteen pepper plants thriving this year, I am once again, for the ninth consecutive year, the largest producer of Hatch chiles in Sauk County, Wisconsin.

References

Leopold, Aldo. 1939. "A Biotic View of Land." *Journal of Forestry* 37 (9): 727.

Leopold, Aldo. 1940. "Wisconsin Wildlife Chronology." *Wisconsin Conservation Bulletin* 5 (11): 6.

O'Keeffe, Georgia. 1976. *Georgia O'Keefe*. New York: Viking.

Shreve, Forrest. 1915. *The Vegetation of a Desert Mountain Range as Conditioned by Climatic Factors*. Washington, D.C.: Carnegie Institution.

Wright, Frank Lloyd. 2005. *Frank Lloyd Wright: An Autobiography*. Petaluma, CA: Pomegranate Communications.

A THOUSAND MILES FROM INHABITED LAND

JAMES ARONSON

As a kid in a white, middle-class suburb of St. Louis, with some friends on our safe street, fortunate to have good enough health, a well-intentioned family, nice pets, a backyard, an alley, and perfectly adequate public schools nearby—I had it good.

But something was deeply amiss, deep inside me, and I did not know what. Starting around age seven or eight and up into my teens I felt deeply out of place, both at home and at school, but I could not see a way out. I was lonely and self-conscious; there was an angry boy in me, too, who had the bad habit of throwing his tennis racket into the net when he missed a shot.

By good luck, there was a pretty marvelous remnant stand of native woodland belonging to a Lutheran seminary five minutes' walk from my house, in a private but accessible landholding just behind our street. It was not wilderness in a deep sense, but it was a door to the outdoors—truly away from people (from a young person's perspective), and it hummed with nonhuman life, of which the best for me was the trees.

At sixteen, I spent a school year abroad, learned a second language, and caught wanderlust. As things worked out, I lived and worked outside the United States for more than forty years, with most of the last thirty years in France. I pursued studies in anthropology, languages, botany, ecology, and—at last—restoration ecology, starting just when that field was taking off.

The title of this essay is a translated quotation from Antoine de Saint-Exupéry.

There, I found an intellectual, vocational, and spiritual way into the world; I also found a community. The biomes where I felt most at home were drylands. Technically, these include deserts and semideserts, or arid and semiarid lands (ASAL), and a piece of each of the Mediterranean-climate regions (MCRs).

In human terms, drylands are places where water is a limiting factor all or almost all year round. Unless a person is well prepared when setting out, this fact may quickly become a matter of life and death for a traveler.

Yet, I still find that I love being far from "inhabited lands," and that, paradoxically, I do not feel lonely there. I have also discovered the fascination of ecotones, or frontier zones, that occur naturally between two adjacent ecosystems, such as those between ASAL and an MCR. There are also beautiful and fascinating ecotones—or life zones—as one goes up from the desert floor to higher elevations in a mountain or mountain range surrounded by desert or embedded within an MCR. Sometimes one side of the mountain is arid and the other is absolutely not. Not surprisingly, the biota in the life zones on the two sides are completely different too.

A good sign of whether people in an area have shown sensitivity, wisdom, and restraint is the presence of clear ecotones—whether gradual or abrupt—at a landscape scale of resolution.

Where people get it wrong, the ecotones tend to disappear. Or, to use the active voice, people have literally *erased* the ecotones. Conversely, in the science and the practice of ecological restoration, one of the best criteria of success is how well we do with the recovery of ecotones.

Let me explain further. Often MCRs are effectively drylands too, with their prolonged periods of annual drought and very high degrees of interannual variability and unpredictability in weather. In fact, some deserts are MCRs, while others have continental-type climates. (The major MCRs are found in central Chile; Baja California, Mexico; the Mediterranean Basin; the Canary Islands; southwestern Australia; and the Cape region of South Africa.)

But the two types of landscapes and ecosystems are different from a human history and ecology perspective—with ASAL generally showing less systematic transformation or destruction at the hands of humans (except in localized mining areas, etc.), while the MCRs are most often more thoroughly remodeled and transformed.

Partly this comes down to where plow agriculture was feasible and where it was not. At their best, however, MCR landscapes not only show ancient and deep human footprints, they also prove that *sometimes* people do get it right: that is, they settle in for generations and use and share resources sustainably, leading to fine-scale spatial patterns and designs of exquisite complexity, based on diverse, synergistic, and partly redundant livelihoods, all contributing to a socioecological ecosystem of the finest ilk.

Coming back to the drylands—their innate mineral and biological wonder and beauty are simply spectacular, especially from the perspective of a naturalist.

I have been truly fortunate. In my day, I have found endless fascination, and moments of awe and pure joy, traveling and observing some of the Earth's most extraordinary plants and animals in drylands, and talking with indigenous people as well as with more recent incomers, who are trying to figure out a gentle way to live on the land and to adapt creatively, and sustainably, in today's crazy and crowded world.

I have also met, and worked with, some of the most imaginative, inventive, hardworking, and inspiring people in the world—those helping damaged dryland ecosystems recover from their "wounds" and come back to health.

In answer to my childhood quest, I found in deserts and semideserts places and communities where people do not seek to be indelibly dominant on the landscapes where they live. Instead, with humility, they act on behalf of diversity, beauty, and wilderness. Maybe it is true that predominantly patriarchal models of civilization need serious revision.

This last year, we reached Earth Overshoot Day on August 18. Next year, it will be a day or three earlier. And this, too, makes me angry, but in a good way. It gives me the desire and the drive to work for restoration, and reeducation, and to help in the transition to sustainability.

And yet, my anger now has a better expression than tennis was for me as an adolescent. I feel that anger in the drylands and MCRs wherever there are continual dust storms due to soil erosion, destruction of biotic crusts, and heedless roadbuilding linked to the maniacal boom-and-bust extraction of mineral, fossil fuel, soil, and vegetable resources.

And there is another thing I have solved. I no longer feel lonely. In all my desert and Mediterranean journeys, I look for special trees, the beautiful and cherished ones, and the ones close enough together to form what we should not hesitate to call desert canopies. I suspect that trees were once far more plentiful in many, many deserts, and that by careful study, with lots of hard work, patience, and love, we could contribute to rebuilding and reweaving the enabling circumstances for some of them.

Innumerable colleagues and comrades have helped shape my sense of urgency to act, to work together, to restore—to fight for something supremely precious and never entirely reparable.

Lately I have been visiting deserts where I had been before, long ago, and some where I have never been. Some are natural ancient deserts, and some are unquestionably human-made ones. To my delight, I have been traveling with my son, Thibaud, who brings along his binoculars and cameras, as well as his love for and deep knowledge of animals.

We make these trips to study and document the real desert trees in their habitats—1,200 and counting—and to interview people doing conservation and restoration work, for a book we are writing (with Edouard Le Floc'h) on desert trees and desert canopies of the world.

I invite you to imagine standing with us beside gargantuan *Euphorbia* trees in drylands of East and southern Africa and Madagascar; or the arborescent cacti of dry intertropical American drylands; or the swollen-trunked *Moringas*, *Sterculias*, *Dracaenas*, *Pachypodiums*, ghost gums, ironwoods, or kejri (*Prosopis*; once widespread in the Middle East and the Thar Desert, today only found in large numbers and size in parts of Rajasthan).

I invite you also to admire otherworldly boojums of the *Fouquieriaceae* in Sonora and Baja California, and their convergent but equally glorious and incongruous counterparts of the *Didiereaceae* of the arid coastal stretch of southwestern Madagascar.

In the Namib Desert, which many consider the oldest desert on Earth, the giant Anabooms, or white acacia trees, still form canopies in the dry riverbeds near the isolated Gobabeb Namib Research Institute. This is remarkable and inspiring. This site doesn't meet Saint Exupéry's high standards of "a thousand miles from any inhabited land," but it is one the most remote desert areas in all of southern Africa and one of the pioneers of desert science research in a region incredibly rich in biota, mystery, and magic. There is also a lot of cumulative degradation, but what is much more surprising and wonderful: a marvelous restoration ecology program at the institute and a start-up master's level training program by and for Namibians. How about that as cause for hope?

DESERT CITY / OCEAN HOME

Five Offerings of Gratitude

ALISON HAWTHORNE DEMING

And never did any science originate but by a poetic perception.
—EMERSON

When I return to the Sonoran Desert after my annual migration to the Canadian Maritimes, I ground myself by planting things. I find this a challenge, though I have lived in Tucson for thirty years. Having grown up in the deciduous forest of New England and spent summers since childhood in Atlantic Canada, my gardening sensibility is attuned to the cycles and seasons of that region. When I first moved to this desert city, I made valiant attempts at growing what I knew how to grow: marigolds, nasturtiums, Oak Leaf lettuce, and Big Boy tomatoes. I pined for lilacs and apple blossoms in spring. I missed maidenhair ferns and the spectacle of scarlet maple leaves in the fall. The desert seemed strange and forbidding. And while the open space of an ocean vista in the north made my spirit expand, the open space of the desert made me feel small and vulnerable. I spent so much time worrying about what I missed that I did not see what was right before my eyes—nature's beauty, inventiveness, and vigor undaunted by conditions of extremity.

After thirty years, I am beginning to understand that the pleasures of gardening in the desert come from learning its vocabulary, not trying to impose my northeast dialect upon the land. So when I returned from the north this year, I visited the local nursery and chose only plants native to arid lands. I chose plants for their aesthetic qualities—candelilla (a.k.a. slipper plants), red yucca, and golden barrel cactus.

Slipper plants look nothing like slippers. They form an elegant cluster of pencil-thick shafts with bright green, thornless, smooth skin. A slipper plant looks like a green parody of a candelabra, thus the Spanish name candelilla, used in its northwest Mexican homelands. I picked two potted candelillas, about two feet tall, growing in a clump about a foot wide, took them home, and slipped them into an oval of rock-rimmed soil where I have previously tried to grow lettuce. Ground squirrels had been grateful that I had put out something for them to nibble, so not many lettuce leaves made it to my table.

Such a ritual of planting is what I do to make myself at home. I get my hands in the dirt and shake my head in wonder at the myriad forms of green intelligence.

I am most grateful for what desert plants teach me about living with aridity and heat. Oddly, they comfort me. They have learned through the time their genetic lineage has spent in harsh environments to be modest and precise in how they meet climatic challenges. No histrionics for these survivors, though some might say the saguaros go a bit over the top in announcing their statuesque presence. But take the candelilla's humble stature and behavior. It does not waste time making leaves or spines or bark. It simply rises up, shafts narrow enough not to lose much water, green enough to make food from the sun.

Candelillas are part of a ridiculously huge and diverse family of plants, the euphorbias, which includes poinsettias, rattlesnake weed, gopher spurge, and devil's backbone, to name only a colorful few. Euphorbs make latex, a milky sap that can quickly heal their wounds. They are named after the ancient Greek physician Euphorbos, who identified a particular euphorb as having laxative properties. The grateful king named the plant after him.

Whether you call them candelillas or slipper plants, their vegetative parts do not look anything like slippers, and they are not slippery. But when they bloom, an eruption of small red flowers tops the stalks, each one looking like a tiny jester's slipper. The plant keeps these slippers a secret until the heat lets it know the time has come to show what it's really made for. I will take comfort watching these plants grow and bloom over the years. I will be as grateful for them as I am for my favorite slippers.

Well, it turns out that one of the other plants I purchased—one labeled "Brakelights Red Yucca"—goes by many names as well, and when not flowering, it looks like a beargrass. No wonder I have suffered confusion over yuccas, agaves, beargrass, sotols, and aloes and still cannot get them straight. I have noticed this grass-like succulent with a tall flowery stalk boasting small bright red waxy blooms growing on median strips in the city. I have admired its tenacity in meager soil and its disregard for the blowback of constant traffic. I have thought, that is an ornamental tough enough to withstand my errors in judgment or care.

Once I accepted that red yucca is not a yucca, I was able to contemplate this lovely plant through what I could observe—its coarse silver-green bladed leaves edged with curling, fibrous threads. I then wondered why it seems to matter so much to know the names, when the names seem blunt instruments in identifying the plants in ways that keep us from really knowing them. Still I am faithful to the task of approximating knowledge of my floral and faunal neighbors. I could go with the precision of scientific names—*Hesperaloe parviflora*, in this case—but would that tell me what I want to know?

I want experiential knowledge. I am grateful for the so-called brakelights red yucca now gracing a corner of my walled backyard. When I step outside, mind racing with obligations and debts and repairs and barely the glimmer of an enticing idea, I stop and stare. I brake for red yucca, and suddenly my cares turn into an ethic of caring.

Golden barrel cactus is native to volcanic slopes in east-central Mexico. It likes to grow at an elevation between 1,400 and 1,900 meters, up above true desert altitudes. In its place of origin, the plant is endangered after years of commercial overcollecting and now by more pervasive threats. Its habitats have been disturbed by dam building and the inundation of desert canyons by reservoirs used for irrigation management.

These days golden barrel cactus, widely cultivated for nurseries, is a grace note to architectural design, a globe-shaped cactus lined with golden spines that make the plant appear to glow as if in a god shine. I have planted mine in a ceramic pot but may have to put it in the ground in a few years. As these plants mature, they grow into a heap of golden globes—a cluster of many that are one.

Let's say then that this cactus stands in for democracy.

Yes, this is a beautiful cactus, the spines radiating out from raised vertical seams in little starburst clusters. But the gorgeous armature is extremely stiff and sharp. The cactus spines form a forbidding defensive weaponry.

Echinocactus grusonii has another misogynistic (the nursery literature calls it "amusing") nickname: mother-in-law's cushion. Is the intent to suggest this is the cushion you would offer to a mother-in-law you hate? Here, have a seat. Or is this the cushion the hated mother-in-law offers, a con job promising comfort while delivering a wound? Oh, was it sharp?—I had no idea. The creepy psychological valence of the nickname is someone's idea of a joke, but it says next to nothing about the plant.

I would call it the Golden Globe cactus because its aesthetic properties are worthy of a major prize. I imagine it on the red carpet: I would like to thank all those who lent a hand in this production.

The desert will always look alien to me, coming as I do from the deciduous woodlands of the northeast. Whenever I fly back home to Tucson, I am stunned by the view over the jet's wing: desiccated terrain spans out, brown and stark. Pathways and deltas, where water once flowed, look like scars running down slopes. Human industry appears corralled—mine, ranch, irrigation circle, testing ground, town, and city. These look like the exception to open space. Brown land. Nothing green in sight.

It is a landscape that might make one ask, Do we belong here? What must we do to be at home in such barren terrain? But, of course, for at least ten thousand years people have belonged to this desert place, they have tended it and abused it, made it flower and let it lie fallow, used its very dirt to build pots and ovens and homes and garden walls. People have matched the desert's inventiveness and skill at surviving extremity.

By the time the jet lands, saguaros, chollas, and ocotillos have raised up their hands in greeting. Scarcity begins, as it does each year for me, to melt away in the presence of the desert's morphological inventiveness. Life in all its entanglements is abundant in the Sonoran Desert, an abundance hard earned in time-crafted adaptations.

Can the desert tolerate *our* abundance, all of us here together with our CSAs and ICE, our Dia de Los Muertos and Large Binocular Telescope, our pecan farms and copper mines, our mescal bacanoras and local brews? Oh, we are as inventive and diverse as nature has taught us to be. But connection—that is the lesson of nature we are trying to learn with our divisions and outrage. How are we connected? How can we be the many that is one? Gratitude for the gift of nature that says, given time and attention and caring, we are fine-tuned, well-oiled, learning machines.

Aristotle's *Physics* speaks of place as a vessel that holds us. To be is to be in a place, yet place is nothing but what it contains. The vessel is a nonentity. It only exists because of what is inside it. We create it out of our need to belong somewhere.

What is place to the young saguaro growing under the shade of its nurse tree? What is place to the bobcat who sharpens his claws on the bottle brush tree in my yard? To the mountain lion who wanders from the Catalina Mountains perhaps as far as the Superstitions, its place a shifting territory of use? To the sharp-shinned hawk that plummets into my yard to take a verdin out of the shrubbery?

We cannot know the mental capacity of these others, but for us, we know that place matters in our world and in our heads. We will fight to the death—of others and even ourselves—to hold a claim on place. A sense of place lets us know we belong.

I see here that I have called to these pages a chorus of voices from science, poetry, and philosophy to interrogate the language we use to speak of the nature of nature in the desert. I want the facts and names, I want the metaphors and feelings, and I want the mind-wandering reflections all to swim together into an appreciation of place and how one comes to feel at home—to land—in an unfamiliar place.

In the springtime, when I return to my ocean home in the Maritimes—a place I have known since childhood—again I am stunned by the view over the jet's wing. This time the astonishment is at green and water. So much! What a verdant planet is this, after all, nothing but forest and meadow and river and lake and stream all gleaming and inviting me to touch down. Yes, the North Atlantic speaks a different language from the Sonoran Desert, but as an antipodal creature, I have learned to appreciate both languages.

Some summer days, when I stare out into the mind-wander of the ocean, I imagine my desert home as it once was, a place where the mountaintops were islands and the desert floor was covered by a sea.

Oh, I am grateful, no matter what the sea threatens here on the edge of peril where we all live, to know this Earth story that tells me that for these moments I belong to a gorgeously unfolding uncertainty.

DESERT AS ART/ECOLOGY NEXUS

ON THE EDGE

Listen to Your Plants

THOMAS M. ANTONIO

When a child asks, "What is the difference between an animal and a plant?," the likely answer will be, "Animals move, and plants do not."

Rooted in place with no immediate mobility, plants develop no central nervous system. What plants do develop is an incredible intimacy with their surroundings. From miles of tiny underground root hairs to leaves floating in a sea of carbon dioxide, spread open to gather sunlight, plants epitomize what it means to be in "the here and now." With a surface-to-volume ratio much higher than that of animals, plants interact with their environment in more ways than most organisms. This is a necessity driven by their need to continually absorb water, sunlight, and carbon dioxide, coupled with their immobility.

For all my life, these silent producers of life-giving oxygen and food have fascinated me.

Long before plant science taught me the difference between a stomata and a stolon, or how to distinguish the chlorophyll green pigment from the carotenoid yellow pigment, I was intrigued by the infinite variety of form, shape, and color in the plant world. All that visual eye candy, and they grow too.

But simply put, plants keep us alive. All life depends on plants. Their importance to us is immeasurable. Unfortunately, by virtue of their ubiquitous nature and their dependability, plants are often ignored and even dismissed. Only their absence or overabundance in an ecosystem brings them into awareness. Regrettably, the steady and reliable growth of these remarkable organisms can make them seem ordinary.

In deserts, however, all life is extraordinary. Perhaps that is why, as a botanist, I enjoy desert habitats. People tend to value what they lack.

In hot, dry, inhospitable climates, even the most cynical have respect for and value how plants can survive. Deserts are not for the faint of heart, especially for members of the vegetable kingdom. There, plants must adapt to various struggles.

Removing a tree that has taken decades to grow in this harsh environment is serious business. Desert plants live on the edge; I have always found people, places, and plants on the edge more captivating. It is the edge that moves one forward. Adaptability is genius, and plants are nothing if not adaptable.

In the natural world, the forms of plants do indeed follow function. Nowhere is that more obvious than in desert plants. It is precisely the characteristics and structures of drought-tolerant plants that display their brilliance.

Living in such dramatically severe places, desert plants have evolved some of the most unique adaptations. Old World, New World, cactus, or euphorbia, their adaptations mirror their environment. Only through close examination, thoughtful inquiry, and timely observation can we truly begin to appreciate these creatures.

Through that heightened sense of observation, viewing desert plants enables my art students from the Institute of American Indian Arts in Santa Fe, New Mexico, to wonder at the ability of art to reveal the truth of nature.

On our field trips in my desert ecology class, these young and gifted indigenous artists fill their journals with drawings of plants whose names are not yet known to them, but whose architecture, color, and texture can still be explored. Millions of years of evolution are made manifest in a protective spine; in the plant's wooly hairs that dissipate the sun's glare while remaining delicate enough to capture dew in the evening; in roots that extend horizontally for hundreds of feet as they probe for water below; in tiny leaves discarded during brutal periods of drought that can quickly grow back when rain descends; and in the green stems that do the bulk of photosynthesis for thick, water-storing leaves and tubers. These structures and strategies are anomalies for most plants living under more mesic conditions.

Then again, it is what we cannot see that maintains life. This ironic truth—made evident through my time with so many artists—is surely a fitting metaphor for our existence. This tenet of science is surely embraced by many forms of art as well. We all need a more imaginative form of observation, for aesthetic interpretations of deserts are no less important than our technical understanding of these places.

We find ourselves drifting further into an economic world that presumes that it can get by with less and less tangible connection to the natural or physical world. Can art bring us back? Surely it can assist. All our senses must be employed if we are to reclaim our proportionate space in nature. Plants can be our mentors, for they have much to teach humankind. It is a pity we are not better pupils, and they are not louder speakers.

EMPTY AND FULL | FAR AND NEAR | ALONE AND TOGETHER

ELLEN MCMAHON

I sat in the dark pickup truck encircled by the cold unfamiliar desert night, my hand in my pocket gently cupped around a warm kangaroo rat. Earlier that day, as our university van descended into the Great Basin, I saw a horizon like I had never seen before, the earth meeting the sky as far as the eye could see—vast flat expanses of reddish brown and grayish green, black buttes and mountains dwarfed by distance.

I was on a field trip with my college biology class to the eastern Oregon desert. We made camp at the base of Hart Mountain and went out in pairs to set live traps to capture some of the small rodents known as kangaroo rats, or "roo rats" for short. Our TA told us excitedly that we were going to go "roo-ratting" as soon as it got dark.

We did not know what that was, but as dusk approached, we split into teams and piled into the back of two pickups. We drove slowly along the rutted roads until we spotted a kangaroo rat hopping along in the glow of the headlights. The driver slammed on the brakes, and we all jumped—or were catapulted—out of the truck.

The idea was to run down and catch the erratically hopping rodent, but in the mad dash and confusion, several of us ended up face down in the dust. Maybe because I was new to the West and visibly awed by this small mammal rodeo, I got to hold the first one we caught.

The more experienced roo ratters suggested I put the rodent in my pocket to keep it calm and warm my hands. The team in the other truck won with seven rats to our two, but I did not care, preoccupied with the intimate connection I felt with my temporary and patient captive. It seems to me now like a pointless and cruel activity, but we were careful to return them to where we originally caught them unharmed and hopefully not too traumatized.

When we went back to check the trap lines we had set earlier in the evening, my partner and I had three kinds of voles, a ground squirrel, a desert pocket gopher, two chipmunks, three kangaroo rats, and several desert mice. We won that competition hands down. In addition to the great number and diversity of small mammals, we saw white pelicans, sandhill cranes, bitterns, herons, avocets, and several species of ducks in the marshy areas along the road.

That weekend blew my mental circuits and reconfigured my mind as it strained to process the paradoxical extremes of the desert. It seemed so dead and barren compared to my forested childhood home, but it was so full of life. The hundreds of miles between towns and ranch houses seemed so lonely, but my experience with the kangaroo rat was the closest encounter I had ever had with a wild animal. And most surprising was the comfort I felt in the harsh landscape. The lonely feeling I had been harboring since childhood did not seem so bad here. Actually, rather than a problem, lonely seemed like the right way to feel in this setting. And I felt a strange kinship with the people living so sparsely distributed in this great expanse of earth and sky.

After graduating from college I spent a few years in the Alvord Desert in eastern Oregon. I worked as a field biologist capturing, documenting, tagging, and sometimes killing small animals for various ecological researchers. One long lonely night while tending my mist nets, I began drawing one of the bats I had captured by the dim light of my headlamp. On the bank of that remote stock pond, to the pungent smell of sagebrush and the distant sounds of wild horses, I realized it was the observation that drew me to biology, not the killing and the counting. This led me to a program in scientific illustration at the University of Arizona in Tucson and to another desert.

Over the last thirty years as a professor in the School of Art, I have not had much opportunity or reason to capture and torment small animals. But I never look out across the Sonoran Desert surrounding my home and think of it as empty, the way I did the first time I saw the Oregon desert.

A few years ago, I followed my tattered field journals back to the study sites in the Oregon desert I had not seen since the 1970s. The bubbling mud pots, white-rimmed mineral ponds, and remote watering holes were just as I remembered them. After the trip I made large gestural paintings and collages attempting to capture the strange compression of time I felt, forty years older in those unchanged places. The paintings were not working for me until I began to notice in the splatters and drips miniature versions of the desert vistas I had seen out my car window on the trip. I cut these out to create a series of tiny landscapes—in the range of one to three inches—that I titled *Distance Passed*.

Even though they look almost photographic, the forms resembling buttes and playas are simply the artifacts of the interactions between ink, paint, charcoal, and paper. The mysterious emergence of these familiar places out of my unintentional mark making suggests to me my biological relationship to the desert. Other people also seem to experience a primordial sort of remembering when they move in close to look at the tiny representations of the vast landscapes.

I had left the Northeast in my early twenties, overwhelmed by the disintegration of my family and the urban chaos and violence of the era. In the desert I found a fruitful disorientation, a renewed sense of wonder, and a fresh way to imagine who I might become. Over the last forty years I've settled into the rich paradoxes of the desert—accepting that emptying my mind of assumptions and expectations helps me to see more clearly, that vast spaces can be more believable at an intimate scale, and that I am just an insignificant midsized mammal who nevertheless has things to do.

A BRIGHT AND SHINING PLACE

STEPHEN TRIMBLE

W*e're going to the desert.* In Salt Lake City, where I live, this is code for heading south to the red rock canyon country of the Colorado Plateau. And yet my friends yearning for slickrock aren't going *to* the desert, they *live* in the desert.

Yes, the Colorado Plateau spanning the Four Corners is dry. It is spacious. Its plants grow from cracks in mesas and adhere to the same modest scale as desert vegetation.

But it's rock that defines this place, not aridity. The canyon country landscape is a lithic declaration by nature, as John Muir said, made "all in one mighty stone word."

The plateau country lies almost completely outside the boundaries of the four North American deserts. So what makes my friends say "desert" when they mean "canyon country"?

Head west or south from the irrigated oasis of our Great Basin Desert city, and the land turns spare. Skies unfurl to infinity. What blurs the boundaries between basin and range desert and Colorado Plateau is the quality of light.

Bunny Fontana used to tell us that in the Tohono O'odham language, the word closest to *desert* is *tohono*, "a bright and shining place." These people of the desert define their home by its light. Parsing the nuances of that light turns out to be devilishly difficult, though I know the gradations are real.

When I moved from the light-struck canyons of the Colorado Plateau to the Sonoran Desert many years ago, I was awed by the blazing intensity of the sun. I've photographed my way through the other North American deserts as well. I'm always aware of the changing light, especially in the Great Basin, where gray-green sagebrush tints the basins and dusty green piñon-juniper woodland colors the mountains. But *gray-green* hardly suffices to contain the multilayered subtlety of the silver-green of sagebrush. One online commentator trying to describe a Honda metallic color called sagebrush pearl settled on "charcoalishlygreenishbluishly metallic." That's not bad.

And how to communicate the color of junipers? Chrysler's juniper green is "the hexadecimal color code #2f4a36 . . . comprising 18.43% red, 29.02% green, and 21.18% blue. This color has an approximate wavelength of 538.15 nm." Not so helpful.

I've looked to physics for clarification. But I soon find myself lost in a matrix of influences on desert light: altitude, latitude, outgassing forests, polluting industry, visual range, relative humidity, haze, aerosols, particulates, scattering molecules, air light, skylight, and ground light.

I know that the clear dry air over the Southwest deserts has much to do with low relative humidity and low haze, allowing for less scattered light and sharp definition of objects—from the chiseled spikiness of Joshua trees silhouetted against the sky to the three-dimensional detail in distant thunderclouds. Higher altitudes and dry desert air extend our visual range to well over a hundred miles.

Still, there's magic in desert light that doesn't yield to simple physical explanation. Scientists have as much to say about how we perceive light, as do the physicists focused on wavelength. Our brains are the deciding factor. Light travels through air and follows all the laws of physics. But color doesn't exist until we see it.

John C. Van Dyke did well in translating this alchemy into words in his 1901 book *The Desert*. Trained as an art historian, he sat on the porch at his brother's ranch in Daggett, California, and pondered what to say about the "almost inexplicable" colors of the Mojave Desert, coming to him through air "so thin, so rarefied; and it is so scentless—I had almost said breathless— that it is like no air at all."

To many, desert air is very easily recognized by the eyes alone: "The traveler in California when he wakes in the morning and glances out of the car-window at the air in the mountain canyons, knowing instantly on which side of the Tehachapi Range the train is moving. He knows he is crossing the Mojave" (Van Dyke 1903).

What Van Dyke is seeing, I think, is the light reflected from the desert itself. No blue snowdrifts or emerald green forest here to cool the color of the air. In the desert, we live with the dun of a desert playa. The reds and ochers of sandstone. The saffron (Van Dyke's word) of summer-cured bunchgrass. And of course in the Great Basin, the aromatic ocean of gray-green sagebrush.

The great naturalist writer Ann Zwinger found the Great Basin a "somber" desert when compared to the hot deserts. She missed "the sunshine of the Mojave, the brilliance of the Sonoran, the glow of the Chihuahuan" (Zwinger 1989). Like the O'odham, Zwinger has resorted to light to define her deserts.

Choose a paint swatch for your desert home. It looks just right on the north wall of your bedroom, a lovely warm neutral cream. Then take that paint chip with you as you travel down the highway. What looked perfect on the bajada of the Catalina Mountains transmogrifies. Your carefully chosen color looks shockingly different as the light shifts with plants and soil.

Downslope, creosote bush sharpens the reflected greens with a biting touch of yellow. Keep driving. The rounded pinkish-gold granitic outcrops of Joshua Tree National Park warm your paint. The shadowed blue of dusk over the Chihuahuan Desert's gypsum dunefield at New Mexico's White Sands makes your neutral bedroom paint as cool as the ocean. Great Basin sagebrush softens and smokes our creamy color. As we travel on through "the sparkling sands of her diamond deserts," we see in color. We breathe in clarity. We live in light. And words really don't suffice.

References

Van Dyke, John C. 1903. *The Desert: Further Studies in Natural Appearances*. New York: Scribner.

Zwinger, Ann. 1989. *The Mysterious Lands*. New York: Dutton.

DESERT SONNET

ANDY WILKINSON

The presence of absence,
all-that's-not creating all-that-is, where
nothing swells to everything, where too much
of too little is more than enough
to open the closed possibilities of the
spoken-for world, where more-is-less
and less-is-more is never better proved
than here within this place of space with
room for every word kept silent, every
vision kept unseen, for every thought and
every feeling kept in hiding 'mongst the
city-swaggered crowd; sky-saturated,
star-complicated, our long horizons
filled with hope of rain.

Rock Martinez and Cristina Perez, *Goddess of Agave* mural. Benjamin Plumbing Supply building, 440 N. 7th Ave., Tucson, Arizona.

Joe Pagac, *Epic Rides* mural. 534 N. Stone Ave., Tucson, Arizona.

Rock Martinez, *Crested Eclipse* mural. Sky Bar, 536 N. 4th Ave., Tucson, Arizona.

Rock Martinez and Fernando Leon, *Plants for the Southwest* mural. 2936 N. Stone Ave., Tucson, Arizona.

Joe Pagac, *Lounging Lizards* mural. 2136 N. Euclid, Tucson, Arizona.

Amir H. Fallah, *Split Screen* mural. MOCA: Museum of Contemporary Art, 265 S. Church Ave., Tucson, Arizona.

Joe Pagac, *Borderlands* mural. North wall of Borderlands Brewery, 119 E. Toole Ave., Tucson, Arizona.

Niki Glen, *Pollinators* mural. N. 5th and E. Toole Ave., Tucson, Arizona.

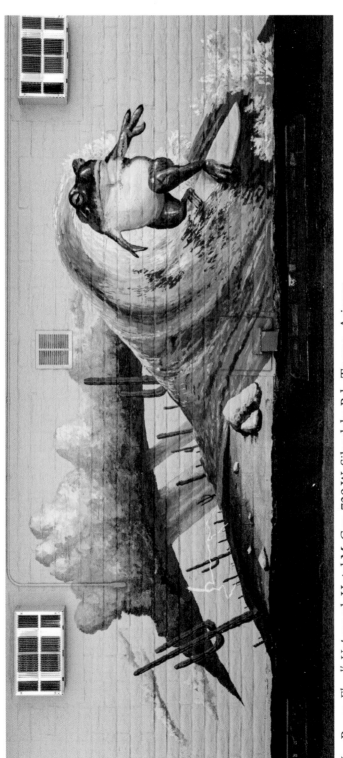

Joe Pagac, *Flood's Up!* mural. Hotel McCoy, 720 W. Silverlake Rd., Tucson, Arizona.

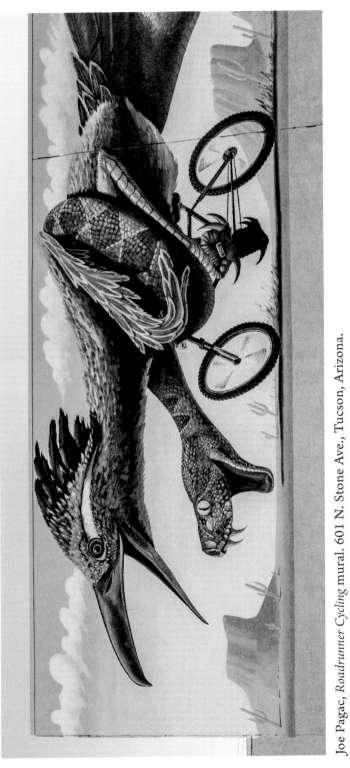

Joe Pagac, *Roadrunner Cycling* mural. 601 N. Stone Ave., Tucson, Arizona.

Isaac Caruso, *Tucson, AZ* mural. 9 N. Scott Ave., Tucson, Arizona.

Lalo Cota, *Desert Heart* mural. 3443 E. Speedway Blvd., Tucson, Arizona.

Joe Pagac, *Sky Islands* mural. 2320 N. Campbell Ave., Tucson, Arizona.

Harriet Wood (Barcelona), *Sonora* mural. 3 Nations Market, 40 W. Brisa St., Ajo, Arizona.

Michael Chiago, *Untitled* mural (detail). 400 W. Vananda Ave., Ajo, Arizona.

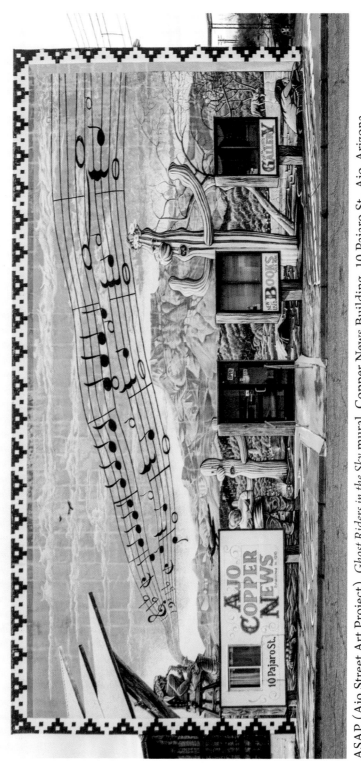

ASAP (Ajo Street Art Project), *Ghost Riders in the Sky* mural. Copper News Building, 10 Pajaro St., Ajo, Arizona.

Leanne C. Miller, *Wild in the Plaza of Memory* mural. Ajo, Arizona.

Unknown artists, *The Lovers* and *Migration*, two murals in Ajo, Arizona.

Michael (DaWolfe) Baker, *Spy Drones Over Sonora* mural. Three Nations Market, Ajo, Arizona.

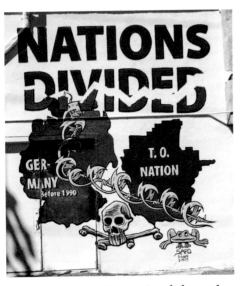

Unknown artist, *Nations Divided* mural, depicting map of Tohono O'odham Nation. Artists Alley, Ajo, Arizona

Amy Juan, *Organpipe Cactus Fruit* mural. Artists Alley, Ajo, Arizona.

Ajo Samaritans, *Humanitarian Aid Is Always Legal* mural (detail). Artists Alley, Ajo, Arizona.

STARING AT THE WALLS

Views of the Desert in Southern Arizona Public Art

PAUL MIROCHA

O ut in the desert, in the middle of nowhere, an ant offers a huge triple-scoop ice cream cone to a drooling Gila monster. A laughing cowboy loses his hat in the dust kicked up by the bucking jackalope he is riding. A lovely señorita stares, euphoric, into space as an agave plant sprouts from her head.

Nearby, another jackalope, a tortoise, and a javelina bounce over rocky ground on bicycles. The barren, saguaro-studded landscape transforms into a woman's long baile folklórico dance skirt. She's riding a bike too, and the full dress flows out behind her in the breeze.

A couple of miles away, four life-size humpback whales float through a desert sky, among towering monsoon storm clouds. The Sonoran Desert landscape below them looks wet, the vegetation glowing in the sunset light.

City dwellers walk, ride, and drive past these images every day. The artwork is supersized, two and three stories tall, painted on the walls of buildings. Such mural art could be an urban scene anywhere, couldn't it? Not likely—there's only one place where people recognize a Gila monster, a jackalope, or a javelina. And where else do they know how to pronounce *saguaro, ocotillo,* or *Gila*? That place is the Sonoran Desert. There's a desert on the edge of town, and it wants to seep quietly into your mind, to remind you where you are.

My first visit to Tucson was like exploring a new planet—coming from Minnesota, this landscape was completely unfamiliar. Yet I felt an immediate attraction. I wanted to walk out into the open landscape and just keep going. Three months later, I drove across the country in a resurrected Econoline van loaded with everything I owned. I arrived in the middle of July. After unpacking a few things, I went for a walk in my new town. I was not sure yet if I wanted to take this place as my home. A bank sign on Speedway Blvd. read 106°F. I had never felt so many photons striking my skin before. Like a rogue wave, it knocked me head over heels. I said to myself, "Yes."

After beginning with a crush, after forty years the relationship is quieter, more mature, I suppose. I've suffered the pain of sunburn, hunger and thirst, heat stroke, being punctured by thorns, the slings and arrows of an uncertain environment. Those things come with the territory, along with the infatuation and the beauty.

I realize, in hindsight, that I nurtured this relationship through drawing. Working as an illustrator, I could keep self-expression in check. Over time, I learned to listen. I painted to let my subjects express themselves. While working, I was outside my own skin, getting under theirs. The secret story of developing this relationship skill is in my sketch books, not the printed pictures people saw.

As I take in the murals in Tucson, I look at them with an eye toward how other artists and their large urban audience perceive the desert as their home. What things do they notice? Have they formed a personal relationship with that environment? Do they dream about it? What stories do desert landscapes tell them?

Wall Art

Painting *and pecking* on walls is a tradition. Humans all over the world have been making petroglyphs and pictographs for at least thirty thousand years (probably longer). It's such a fundamental human behavior, surely we can tell something about those people by what they painted on their walls. We don't know exactly what ancient cave paintings meant to their creators, but we respond to them because we are equally human, wired exactly the same.

Many of these unknown painters and etchers were excellent observers of the natural world. Iconic animal and plant species are often recognizable. Other life forms in these works are fantastic, fanciful, or mythological. The meanings—stories, symbols, and memes—understood at the time are *obscured*. I would love to interview those ancient artists and their audiences if I could, yet their work stands on its own. It is useful to look at this art as such, apart from the intentions of its creators.

Wall art is of its own time. It conveys ideas current during the period in which it was created. Murals don't last long as walls crumble and paint fades. Several of the murals I consider in this chapter have already disappeared, possibly painted over.

In the recent past, Tucson's public murals were most common in Mexican and Native American neighborhoods. In the last ten years or so, murals have moved out of the Mexican barrios in metro Tucson and can be seen almost anywhere, notably downtown. They seem to proliferate where people from different cultures mix. It's not surprising to see that they still riff off traditional Mesoamerican icons: Our Lady of Guadalupe, mariachis, gorgeous Latina ladies in costume, Day of the Dead icons, Aztec warriors. Diego Rivera dances with Frida Kahlo on one Tucson wall. But the inventory of images is evolving rapidly beyond that tradition.

Public art is free and visible to everyone. It's democratic and gains its creative power from being multicultural. By its existence and widespread acclaim, public art, in a sense, has been voted on.

We can, therefore, speculate that art in public spaces enjoys a level of shared meaning among locals. The ant and the Gila monster may only generate a passing smile. But as we pass them frequently, the images remain with us as riddles. Images are food for the brain. Maybe it's the mind trying to figure out the story line, or if there is one.

Even in an urban environment, a milieu made over for human use, one can't ignore the surrounding landscape. It's a factor in an urban dweller's life. Many native plants and animals cross our city limits and thrive here. So does the weather. On arriving or leaving town, by air or by highway, one is struck by the pure physical presence of the natural landscape looming to the horizon. Maps fix city limits, but the boundaries are permeable. Like Gila woodpeckers on our telephone poles, desert images filter into public art and into our minds.

A collection of mural images might tell a thoughtful observer something about how urban desert dwellers view the surrounding natural environment. How do people of my time imagine the Sonoran Desert?

The Desert as Home

What does it mean to live in a desert and to call it home?
"The sense of home is not the culture, not the food, not even the many relatives," writes the late Native American author Viola F. Cordova (2007). "It is the place: the look of the early morning; the smell of the juniper; the particular expected temperature for the kind of day it is, for the time of year it is; the mountains being in the right place." Cordova, a philosophy professor of mixed Jicarilla Apache/Hispanic descent, wrote these lines to define an indigenous sense of place. She addressed the eternal questions of Western philosophy from her own cultural point of view. What is the world? Who are we? What should we do in this particular world we have been born into?

Native peoples, she says, have a need to identify with a specific bounded space. Belonging to a place defines who that person is. One feels at home there, safe, surrounded by familiar things. In this view, the landscape of home is an extension of personal space, intimate as a body part, as much a part of you as the neurons in your brain, or your dreams. "When you dream, you go to a place in nature," wrote Yoeme (Yaqui) poet Refugio Savala (1980).

Do you have to be indigenous, or born and raised in a place, to feel such emotional attachments to it? Do immigrants and refugees, then, have a much more shallow relationship with the place in which they are currently living?

The southern Arizona stretch of the Sonoran Desert is a good place to find out. In this desert, on both sides of the U.S.-Mexico border, we see a very mobile population today.

To be sure, people have come to the Sonoran Desert from every type of environment on Earth. Even the Native Americans living here might be from Alaska or other contrasting environments. A good part of the population is seasonal, spending only the winters here. Gary Nabhan is from the dunes along Lake Michigan's shore of Gary, Indiana, and I grew up in St. Paul,

Minnesota, each from our namesake towns. But we both call the Sonoran Desert our home of homes.

We all respond differently to images. Most of that response is visceral; there's no single correct or rational viewpoint. And yet images can reveal their own internal coherence, reflecting minds of both the artists and their audience. Key trends and themes may emerge about attitudes and states of mind that would otherwise be invisible.

To learn more, I surveyed street murals in two desert cities, Tucson and Ajo, Arizona. These are several of the questions I asked as Gary and I drove around, surveying the public art in these two desert cities.

- What kind of emotional attachments do we have to our space, bounded by mountains?
- How do we visualize what's going on out there, if anything is?
- Do citizens of different cities view their surroundings differently?
- How much desert ecology do citizens understand?
- Do themes of scarcity or plenty predominate in desert paintings?

To answer these questions, I searched for panels that depicted landscape elements and photographed them. I chose fifty panels from Tucson and thirty-five from Ajo to show to a group of observers so that we could process the images together. I instructed them to imagine they were alien explorers or archaeologists from the future, a thousand years from now. These are the major motifs we inventoried, the cast of characters in the collective dream we call the Sonoran Desert.

Views of the Landscape

Landscape view was my main criterion in choosing the murals to consider. I found two dominant subgroups: idealized Sonoran Desert landscapes and scenes from other environments. There were several important images of the ocean. They remind us that the Sonoran Desert is essentially a horseshoe surrounding the Sea of Cortés. Though the ocean seems to be the opposite of a desert, the two form a point and counterpoint. Most of the "exotic landscapes" depict tropical scenes. Sometimes saguaro cacti and palm trees exist in the same scene. Native *Washingtonia* palms and Old World *Phoenix* date palms are commonly planted in the urban landscape. But these painted palms near oceans look more like coconut palms. The combination of desert and tropical plants expresses both a feeling of abundance bursting with life and peaceful relaxing feelings.

To a biogeographer, there is an underlying truth in this blending of desert and tropics. Tucson is on the northern edge of the Sonoran Desert. If you want to truly know the place, you cross into Sonora and you can see the gradual increase in biodiversity. From southern Sonora you can watch the reverse happen as you travel north. Indeed, the Sonoran Desert flora evolved from southern tropical plants. As botanist Tom Van Devender (n.d.) put it, the tropical deciduous forest is the "grandmother" of the Sonoran Desert.

Among Sonoran Desert landscapes, I found several subgroups, as well. In some scenes I call hybrids, saguaros grow in a barren desert clearly akin to the Colorado Plateau of northern Arizona and Utah. Such hybrid deserts have been shaped at least as far back as the filming of *The Petrified Forest* in 1936. There, Bette Davis and Humphrey Bogart meet in the northern Arizona Painted Desert, replete with saguaro mannequins. This could be a result of scientific confusion, or an expressive way to show a stylized desert of rocks and mountains, part of the artist's vision.

I am curious that some of the landscapes show lush green vegetation, while others have lots of dry space between plants. Tucson resides in the Arizona upland subdivision of the Sonoran Desert, a relatively moist place, almost not a "real" desert. So where did these images of barrenness come from? Maybe they are faster to paint. Or do they come from memories of driving through the mesmerizing emptiness of the hundred-mile stretch on I-10 between Tucson and Phoenix? Covered with abandoned farmland, this area wasn't always this way. Now it is the source of huge haboob dust storms, which have covered Phoenix in a layer of dust like snow.

Mountains

More than half of the murals surveyed (about 60 percent) have mountains in the background, usually paired with a sunset. The mountains in four directions are a fundamental reminder of the surrounding landscape. They are visible from everywhere in Tucson, and from most other Sonoran Desert cities. Mountains show above the buildings and remind us where we are. Everyone uses the mountains as landmarks for navigating the streets in town.

Dust

It's usually dry here, and sometimes windy. Humans have taken out a lot of plant cover. The walls show cattle, horses, and a jackalope kicking up the dust. Dust is a familiar visual, olfactory, and even taste sensation to every desert dweller. It's a thing, as every resident who dusts the shelves in their house will nod in agreement.

Knowing the Names

Names are important. We humans begin our relationships by learning each others' names. Remembering the names of plants and animals is also a measure of intimacy with our surroundings. It's not just science—it's common courtesy. Recognizing the names of plants as I walk a familiar desert path is like greeting longtime friends. Knowing their names shows respect. And I'd swear that I receive a quiet friendly response. I'm curious about the names I don't yet know. I anticipate learning a new plant's job, its perspective on the world, and where I'm likely to find it again. Once I do that, I start to see that plant everywhere.

When I was traveling in Malaysia, people explained a simple saying they had, "*Tak kenal—tak cinta*," literally, "Don't know—don't love." There is love at first sight, but long, continuing love is nourished by constant efforts to "know" through all the senses. Since there is no end to knowing, there are no boundaries on love. The murals are efforts to more deeply know relationships between species as symbols of beauty and symbiosis.

Saguaros and prickly pear cacti far outnumber other plants in both cities. Barrel cacti, palo verdes, ocotillos, bursages, agaves, and jimsonweeds are likewise familiar characters. It's no surprise that saguaros, the defining species of the Sonoran Desert—as well as the icon—came in first. Prickly pear cacti were present everywhere, bursting with moisture, colorful fruits, and flowers. Ajo residents seemed to know more plant species. This is suggested by accurate images of a saguaro flower, an organ pipe cactus fruit, a desert lavender plant. A night-blooming cereus had something to say—it is emerging from an electronic megaphone, its moth pollinator on a wall nearby.

I searched the paintings for evidence of deeper understandings. A toad surfing on a monsoon flash flood shows a humorous understanding of how storms wake the toads from their underground torpor so they can come out and party.

A more complex example is seeing the plant associations in a landscape. I looked for the bursage plant in company with palo verde trees and saguaros. The small, humble (but not ugly) bursage is largely responsible for the presence of saguaros. Typically, bursage, being bad-tasting, hides tasty seeds from rodents. It's a nurse plant for the germinating palo verde tree, which in turn shelters young saguaros. This triad of plants interact to create a distinct texture found nowhere else, with infinite variations. Like a piece of music, the landscape plays variations on the same themes over the centuries, always different, yet recognizable as home. Leaving out a plant is like removing a note from a symphony.

In Tucson's regionally renowned Farmer John's meat plant mural, I saw the bursages and saguaros, but no palo verdes. This might seem overly picky on my part, but it explains some of the joy I felt when I finally found O'odham artist Michael Chiago's work, hidden behind the Curley School in Ajo. The landscape is painted carefully, like a portrait of a well-known friend. O'odham people are shown in a landscape carefully observed, with everything in its place. There are the little bursage bushes, palo verdes, and saguaros. The vast emptiness of the landscape is satuarated with both knowledge and love. The sense of being at home, safe, in a familiar place is palpable.

Mythical and Whimsical Desert Animals

The preponderance of these images reflects the artist's way of seeing things, especially in the murals of Joe Pagac. One of my observers exclaimed, "Right whales in the wrong place," on seeing the image of Joe's levitating leviathans floating among huge monsoon cumulus clouds above a recently watered desert.

At first glance, it is surreal, yes, but it also illustrates a great truth known to desert dwellers from around here. The water from the great monsoon storms provides half a year's rainfall. The storms on which everything depends come from the Gulf of California. Why not blow the whales along with them?

The desert outside town appears to be an enchanted place. There, mythical animals and plants appear as if in dreams, imagination, and visions.

Two murals in Ajo illustrate this well—the *Singing Saguaros* mural (with musical notes playing "Ghost Riders in the Sky") and the *Night of the Lepus* panel, inspired by a 1972 sci-fi movie about killer rabbits that was filmed here.

Goddess Figures

I don't know how better to describe this motif. These beauties are encountered often enough on the walls to deserve their own category. There is a similar look and pose—she looks up and away with a euphoric expression—and always with something colorful or energetic surrounding her face, perhaps an agave, flowers, swirling hair, and more.

The agave woman on the walls of Tucson's Benjamin Supply building is the Mexican agave goddess, Mayahuel, well-known even in these northern parts. She is one of several mother and fertility goddesses in Aztec spirituality, a personification of beauty, nourishment, and fruitfulness. She is also the artist's girlfriend. The image is riveting, hot and spicy as heck.

Color

My fellow observers saw mural colors as "terrific, striking, prismatic, powerful, lush, tropical, psychedelic." Several intense colors are aptly observed and come from the surrounding landscape, but you don't see them everywhere. The overall palette of the desert landscape is muted, neutral tones. Bright colors usually occur in small patches, or if covering the landscape, only for limited and often unpredictable flowering periods. An exception to this is the desert sunset, which covers the whole sky and illuminates the land below it every day, no two ever the same.

An infinite gradation of grays and browns in a vast space is a perfect context for the appreciation of these hotspots of intense chroma. In the urban environment, the murals stand out in roughly the same way, spots of brilliant color surrounded by mostly muted tones.

There is more *green* in the Midwest where I grew up, but more *greens* in the Sonoran Desert—desert greens are more varied and numerous. Although the Sonoran Desert typically has the grayed-down greens of saguaros, palo verdes, and bursage, I prefer to call these greens complex. Each plant has its own spectral signature. For an artist, a walk in the desert is like being at a wine tasting. A few of the most delicious flavors are so subtle, it takes time to develop the sight to distinguish them. The palette is rich.

The murals embrace the lively color palette of Mexico, originating with the indigenous peoples. This color dimension is so prevalent that one may forget its ancient origins in this region. As linguist Jane Hill (1992) explained it in her article "The Flower World of Old Uto-Aztecan," the strong use of color itself is a powerful cultural symbol. Hill writes, "A complex system of spirituality, centered on metaphors of flowers, is part of the cultural repertoire of many of the prehistoric and historic peoples of the Southwest and Mesoamerica."

Flowers, iridescent hummingbirds, and butterflies offer us the see-through freshness of light through water and the prismatic color of sunsets. These are places where the spiritual world temporarily pokes through the veil between worlds into ours, which is painted in shades of gray. The Aztecs described several paradises in the afterlife, filled with flowers, butterflies, birds, light, and lush color. They inherited this from a tradition going back for millennia. Present desert dwellers inherited it quietly from these same roots. Maybe some of us simply noticed the same patterns the ancients did.

To a desert dweller, the connection between rain, flowers, and color is clear. Spectacular desert blooms are triggered by the rains, and good times follow. The Yoeme (Yaqui) Deer Dancer is an iconic cultural image found in Tucson murals. Using ritual dance, the Deer Dancer goes to *sea ania*, the flower world. It's a spiritual place of brilliant light and color, where he becomes the spirit of the deer. In Felipe Molina and Larry Evers's book *Yaqui Deer Songs* (1987), they describe the enchanted flower world as "a perfected mirror of all the beauty of the natural world of the Sonoran Desert." A mural, now gone, *The Fall of the Yaqui Deer Dancer*, at Old Pascua in Tucson, thrilled thousands of visitors who revered it as a shrine.

Nations and Borders

If I had studied the murals from Tucson and Ajo without a map, I would still guess that Ajo is closer to Mexico and to the Tohono O'odham Nation. Indeed, Ajo, Arizona, is forty-three miles from the border at Sonoyta, Sonora, and a few miles from the western edge of the main O'odham reservation. Tucson is sixty-six miles north of the border, but location counts for a lot. Organ Pipe National Monument and the highway from Sonoyta are major immigration routes. A mural in Tucson depicts various desert animals standing, confused, at the border wall. But these issues take on added urgency 130 miles to the west. That's why Ajo has its own categories—the border and the O'odham.

"This is Hia-ced O'odham country," a sign reads. These western kin to the Tohono O'odham, also called Areneños, Sand Dune People (formerly Sand Papagos), live in this area without an official reservation. Three cultures mix here, and it shows in public art. Several murals express solidarity between American citizens—both indigenous people and immigrants—and the migrant border crossers from the south.

The murals tell the stories of how the border affects the Tohono O'odham Nation as well as migrants from Mexico. The U.S.-Mexico border divides traditional O'odham land, separating families. One panel in Ajo uses maps of the reservation and divided Germany before 1990, when the Berlin wall came down, to compare the seriousness of the issue. The border is depicted on the map by razor wire. Another mural, *Humanitarian Aid Is Always Legal*, depicts a jug of water, cans of food, and first aid. They go beyond mere symbols—a real jug of water and a crate of canned food are placed next to the mural. Service, first aid, safety for the homeless are offered in the heart of the desert.

Butterflies

Lepidopterans occur on the Tucson walls, but they are a more focused theme in Ajo, especially the monarch butterfly, which migrates annually from North America to southern Mexico. Several images show people turning into butterflies. The monarch is adopted by DACA (Deferred Action of Childhood Arrivals) youth, immigrants, and refugees as a symbol of resilience. In one panel, immigrants trek across a map of North America, walking toward a labeled "Freedom Bus." To me this is a direct reference to the Freedom Riders of Alabama in the 1960s. Moths, the nocturnal cousin to butterflies, were also found on Ajo walls—hawkmoths, the forgotten pollinators of the *Datura* flower in a Tucson mural.

The Sun

Brilliant yellows and oranges in these murals are a frequent background motif, often set off by a deep blue background. This color contrast of bright oranges and dark blues is a common element in the palettes of desert muralists. Nearly everyone loves the postcard desert sunsets. Again, the significance of color runs deeper, embedded in traditional stories. In Ruth Underhill's book about living with the O'odham in the Sonoran Desert, *People of the Crimson Evening*, she describes how Elder Brother created the Desert People from clay and gave them the Crimson Evening (1951). Along with life and a place to live, the Creator gave them enough beauty to light up the landscape. That exact crimson is a difficult color to mix with pigments. Many artists, like me, have tried to paint that unpaintable light.

Hearts

There are enough hearts in the murals in both cities to give them meme status. The heart is the seat of spiritual and physical well-being. It symbolizes love, eros, and emotional connection—the center. The heart contrasts with the intellectual and linear thinking symbolized by the brain. In Ajo, a painted heart is literally labeled, "Heart of the Sonoran Desert." In one Tucson mural, columnar cacti grow like blood vessels from an anatomical heart. In another by the same artist, a pair of lungs grow into a tree. "Trees are the lungs of the desert," notes one of our observers. True, the oxygen we breathe comes from trees.

The heart images growing from desert landscape elements suggest that many people want to feel a relationship there, as if the desert is a person. Maybe that signifies the blending of the landscape with personal space described so well by Viola Cordova. One message on a Tucson mural says, "I love where I live." That creates a paradox, for many city dwellers seem to focus on the desert as an oasis, not as what the common definition of a desert implies—"a barren area with living conditions hostile for plant and animal life." It is truly loved for the richness it *has*, not for what is lacking.

To some, deserts may still seem inhospitable, but the Sonoran Desert we see in these murals is an enchanted place, a place of imagination. Surprise appearances happen. You may see a jackalope out there, a gorgeous goddess, or a Gila monster.

For over a century, Tucson has had the help of the Desert Laboratory on Tumamoc Hill in becoming desert smart. Perched on the side of a mountain overlooking the city like an acropolis, the Desert Laboratory was the first field station in the world dedicated entirely to the study of arid environments. Researchers there mapped the natural boundaries and produced the first binational, ecoregional flora—that's a list of plant names, part census and part family tree. That work began in 1903, yet it has helped the Old Pueblo community imagine the Sonoran Desert in a way that continues to this day. As the Desert Lab's former director Forrest Shreve once waxed eloquently (1931),

> The most significant lesson that the desert dweller can learn from a familiarity with its plant and animal life is to regard himself not as an exile from a better place, but at home in an environment to which his life can be adjusted without physical or intellectual loss.

Some contemporary desert muralists are willing to go a bit further than that, and so am I. We are not just avoiding loss. We are looking a little deeper—through the prickly façade and past the gray-brown leaves that are only playing dead. And when we do, we see that the desert is both sensuous and succulent—it's downright juicy out there.

References

Cordova, V. F. 2007. *How It Is: The Native American Philosophy of V. F. Cordova.* Tucson: University of Arizona Press.

Evers, L., and F. S. Felipe. 1987. *Yaqui Deer Songs/Maso Bwikam: A Native American Poetry.* Tucson: University of Arizona Press.

Hill, J. 1992. "The Flower World of Old Uto-Aztecan." *Journal of Anthropological Research* 48 (2): 117–44.

Savala, R. 1980. *Autobiography of a Yaqui Poet.* Tucson: University of Arizona Press.

Shreve, F. 1931. *The Cactus and Its Home.* Baltimore, MD: Williams and Wilkins.

Underhill, R. M. 1951. *People of the Crimson Evening.* Washington, D.C.: U.S. Department of the Interior, Bureau of Indian Affairs, Branch of Education.

Van Devender, T. R. n.d. *The Deep History of the Sonoran Desert.* Accessed June 22, 2020. https://www.desertmuseum.org/books/nhsd_deep_history.php.

CONTRIBUTORS

Thomas M. Antonio is co-author of *The Sunflower Family in the Upper Midwest* and has served as associate professor and science coordinator at the Institute of American Indian Arts, where he spearheaded a seed library project as director for the USDA Equity Grants Program at IAIA. He has also worked for the Chicago Botanic Garden and as curator of collections for Garfield Park and Lincoln Park Conservatories.

Homero Aridjis is regarded as one of Latin America's greatest living writers and is celebrated for his pioneering work as an environmental activist. He served two terms as president of PEN International. Many of his fifty books of poetry and prose have been translated into fifteen languages, and he has been awarded important literary and environmental prizes in Mexico, France, Italy, the United States, and Serbia. He has been Mexico's ambassador to Switzerland, the Netherlands, and UNESCO. His most recent books in English are *News of the Earth, Maria the Monarch*, and *The Child Poet*.

James Aronson is senior scientist at Restoration Ecology Center for Conservation and Sustainable Development at Missouri Botanical Garden. His interests include the intermingling of the sciences, ethics, philosophy, and policy aspects of ecological restoration. He has a special long-standing interest in the evolutionary and community ecology, systematics, and biogeography of trees native to arid, semiarid, and Mediterranean-climate regions. He is co-author of several books and has contributed numerous articles and chapters to dozens of journals and anthologies. He earned a PhD at the Hebrew University of Jerusalem in 1990.

Tessa Bielecki co-founded the Spiritual Life Institute and lived there as monk and Mother Abbess for almost forty years. In 2005, she co-founded the Desert Foundation as an informal circle of friends who explore the wisdom of the world's deserts, focusing on peace and understanding between the three Abrahamic traditions. Tessa was one of the first teachers at Naropa University's Buddhist-Christian dialogue in the 1980s, an experience that she calls pivotal in her life. She is recognized as one of the foremost scholars of St. Teresa de Avila, and she is the author of several books and CDs on the mystic saint, including the recently recorded *Wild at Heart* for Sounds True. She teaches at Colorado College, gives lectures and retreats, and participates in East-West dialogues.

Alberto Búrquez currently works at the Instituto de Ecología, Department of Ecology of Biodiversity, Universidad Nacional Autónoma de México. He researches in ecology, evolutionary biology, and ethnoecology. He earned his PhD from the Department of Zoology at the University of Cambridge in 1988, and he co-edited and authored much of a landmark book in Spanish on the natural and cultural history of the Sonoran Desert region, *Complejos Bioculturales de Sonora: Pueblos y Territorios Indígenas*.

Francisco Cantú served as an agent for the United States Border Patrol from 2008 to 2012, working in the deserts of Arizona, New Mexico, and Texas. This experience served as the foundation for his memoir, *The Line Becomes a River: Dispatches from the Border* (Riverhead Books, 2018), winner of the 2017 Whiting Award for nonfiction. He is a former Fulbright Fellow and the recipient of a Pushcart Prize and a 2018 Art for Justice fellowship. His writing and translations have been featured in *Best American Essays, Harper's, n+1, Orion,* and *Guernica,* as well as on *This American Life.* He lives in Tucson.

Douglas Christie received his his MA from Oxford University and his PhD from the Graduate Theological Union. He has been awarded fellowships from the Luce

Foundation, the Lilly Foundation, and the NEH. From 2013 to 2015 he served as co-director of the Casa de la Mateada study abroad program in Córdoba, Argentina. His primary research interests focus on contemplative thought and practice in Christianity and on spiritual ecology. He is the author of *The Word in The Desert: Scripture and the Quest for Holiness in Early Christian Monasticism* and *The Blue Sapphire of the Mind: Note for a Contemplative Ecology*, and he is the founding editor of *Spiritus: A Journal of Christian Spirituality*.

Paul Dayton is a marine ecologist who was bred, born, and belongs in the Sonoran Desert. He is a professor emeritus of oceanography in the Integrative Oceanography Division at Scripps Institution of Oceanography, University of California, San Diego. He has conducted investigations in several parts of the world, including spending fifty months in Antarctica, performing research during more than five hundred dives under the ice. His career has been motivated by the belief that one must understand nature to protect it. For such work, Dayton has received the E. O. Wilson Naturalist Award and the Ramon Margalef Prize, plus a lifetime achievement award from the Western Society of Naturalists.

Alison Hawthorne Deming is an author of poetry and nonfiction. She is the Agnese Nelms Haury Chair of Environment and Social Justice, a professor of creative writing, and a Regents Professor at the University of Arizona. Her most recent books are the poetry collection *Stairway to Heaven* and *Death Valley: Painted Light*, a collaboration with photographer Stephen Strom. Deming received an MFA from Vermont College, a Wallace Stegner Fellowship from Stanford University, and numerous poetry fellowships. Her work has been awarded the Pablo Neruda Prize from Nimrod, Pushcart Prize, Gertrude B. Claytor Award from the Poetry Society of America, Best Essay Gold Award from the GAMMA Southeastern Magazine Association, and Bayer Award in Science Writing for Creative Nonfiction.

Father David Denny is a desert contemplative, poet, and editor whose work has explored desert spiritual traditions in the Middle East, Central Asia, and North Africa. A native of Indiana, Denny moved to Arizona in 1969, where he attended Prescott College, studied Arabic in Libya, and graduated from the University of Arizona. Ordained a Roman Catholic priest in 1980, he served monastic communities in Nova Scotia and Colorado while also being engaged in Christian-Muslim dialogues. Recently returned to Arizona, he is the executive co-director of the Desert Foundation and outreach priest for Cross Catholic Outreach. His poetry has appeared in the *Desert Call*.

Exequiel Ezcurra is an innovative plant ecologist who has been honored worldwide for his contributions both as an academic and as an active conservationist. He served as director of the University of California's UC/MEXUS and as a professor of plant ecology with University of Callifornia, Riverside's Department of Botany and Plant Sciences. Ezcurra came to UC/MEXUS from the San Diego natural science and research program. For four years, he served as president of the National Institute of Ecology in Mexico and was then appointed director general of SEMARNAT, the natural resources and conservation secretariat of the Mexican federal government. His classic environmental history, *The Basin of Mexico*, is available in numerous editions and translations.

Thomas Lowe Fleischner is the executive director of a newly independent nonprofit version of the Natural History Institute. He recently transitioned to faculty emeritus status at Prescott College, where he taught in the interdisciplinary Environmental Studies Program for twenty-nine years. In addition to helping coordinate the conservation biology and natural history and ecology emphasis areas, he created courses that linked with many other curricular areas, including creative writing, environmental politics, and ecopsychology. Most recently he edited *Nature, Love, Medicine: Essays on Wildness and Wellness*.

Jack Loeffler is an aural historian, songcatcher, radio producer, writer, and jazz musician. From co-founding the Black Mesa Defense Fund to attending the first global conference on the environment in Stockholm in 1972, he has been at the cutting edge of environmental action and ecological thought. Among his five books are *Adventures with Ed: A Portrait of Abbey* and *Healing the West: Voices of Culture and Habitat*. He is affectionately known as the Studs Terkel of southwestern counterculture, having interviewed, dialogued, and camped with the likes of Ed Abbey, Estevan Arrellano, Peter Coyote, Dave Foreman, Sylvia Rodriguez, Terry Tempest Williams, Rita Swentzell, and Gary Snyder.

Ellen McMahon is a professor in the School of Art at the University of Arizona. She has an MS in scientific illustration from the University of Arizona and an MFA in visual art from Vermont College of Fine Art. In 2007, she received a Fulbright Scholar's grant for a six-month stay in Puerto Peñasco, Mexico, with the Center for the Study of Deserts and Oceans. In 2010, she initiated and served as project director and co-editor of a research project addressing the fragile aqueous ecology of the southwestern United States. This project culminated in the book *Ground | Water: The Art, Design and Science of a Dry River*.

Rubén Martínez, an Emmy-winning journalist and poet, is the author of *Crossing Over: A Mexican Family on the Migrant Trail*, *The New Americans*, and more. He lives in Los Angeles, where he holds the Fletcher Jones Chair in Literature and Writing at Loyola Marymount University. Many contributors in this book consider Martínez's *Desert America* to be the finest social history of the multicultural Southwest ever written.

Curt Meine is a conservation biologist, historian, film narrator, and writer. He received his bachelor's degree in English and history from DePaul University in Chicago and his graduate degrees in land resources from the Nelson Institute for Environmental Studies at the University of Wisconsin–Madison. He has written the definitive biographies of Aldo Leopold and Wallace Stegner, and he is the guide to the legacy of the Leopold family in the documentary film *Green Fire*. He serves on the boards of numerous conservation and restoration nonprofits.

Alberto Mellado Moreno is a Comcáac (Seri) indigenous leader from Socaaix, Punta Chueca, Sonora, in Mexico. A marine scientist with aquacultural expertise and a conservation professional for over fifteen years, he also serves his indigenous community as a local historian, creative writer, artisan, and husband and father. His trilogy *Los Comcáac: Una Historia Narrativa* is the first-ever documentary of the Comcáac history since Spanish contact written by a tribal member.

Paul Mirocha is a designer and an illustrator, inspired by science, and interested in how humans perceive their surroundings. He is an artist-in-residence at the University of Arizona's Desert Laboratory on Tumamoc Hill. His posters, book illustrations, and prints have set the standards for desert natural history illustrations since 1985. They have adorned the covers of novels and natural histories by the likes of Barbara Kingsolver, Stephen Buchmann, Gary Paul Nabhan, and Janice Bowers for four decades. His mandolin playing is just as artful and exuberant.

Gary Paul Nabhan is known as a plant conservationist, desert ecologist, and nature writer. He is also an Ecumenical Franciscan Brother immersed in desert spiritual traditions, in building cross-cultural collaborations, and in facilitating border justice and food justice initiatives. His scientific focus on desert nurse plant ecology has led to the designation of Ironwood Forest National Monument and the Rock Corral Canyon Wild Chile Reserve. As a Lebanese-American grandson of refugees, he has been engaged in interfaith peacemaking, sacred site restoration, and refugee farmworker activism. He has been honored by the MacArthur Foundation with a "genius" fellowship and by Utne Reader as a "world visionary."

Ray Pierotti is associate professor of ecology and evolutionary biology at University of Kansas. A native of New Mexico, Pierotti has long been a keen observer of the interactions among different species of mammals, reptiles, and birds in the American West. His research investigates the evolutionary biology of vertebrates with male parental care and socially monogamous breeding systems. He has spent time in the field in Arizona and Sonora as well.

Larry Stevens is an evolutionary ecologist and the curator of ecology at the Museum of Northern Arizona in Flagstaff, where he also serves as director of MNA's Springs Stewardship Institute. He also co-founded the Grand Canyon Wildlands Council and played a key role in proposing and demarcating national monuments on the Colorado Plateau. Over the past half century he has studied the ecology of the world's most famous large deep canyon, and the river that carved it, working as a river guide and for the National Park Service, the Bureau of Reclamation, the Department of the Interior, several colleges and universities, and Grand Canyon Wildlands Council. In addition, he is an accomplished painter, musician, whitewater rafter, and songwriter.

Stephen Trimble is an award-winning nature photographer and writer who has taught in the Honors College and Environmental Humanities Program at the University of Utah, where he spent a year as a Wallace Stegner Centennial Fellow. Author of a dozen books, Trimble co-edited the essay collection *Testimony: Writers of the West Speak on Behalf of Utah Wilderness*. He also edited *Red Rock Stories: Three Generations of Writers Speak on Behalf of Utah's Public Lands*. Trimble serves as a consultant and writer for the conservation community, including the Nature Conservancy's Colorado Plateau Conservation Initiative.

Octaviana V. Trujillo (Yaqui) is founding chair and professor in the Department of Applied Indigenous Studies at Northern Arizona University and teaches courses on tribal nation building. A primary focus of her work as a former chairwoman of the Pascua Yaqui Tribe has been developing programs that provide the use of her academic and indigenous knowledge for promoting environmental and social justice. Co-author of the *Sacred Lands and Gathering Grounds Toolkit,* she has played a lead role in the Healing the Border Project of the Alianza Indigena sin Fronteras.

Benjamin T. Wilder's research is broadly focused in desert ecology and botany. He uses multiple approaches to establish baselines to better understand modern biodiversity and connect science to conservation. Since October 2016 he has been the acting director of the Desert Laboratory on Tumamoc Hill. He also works with Dr. Christopher Scott in the administration of CAZMEX, the Consortium for Arizona-Mexico Arid Environments. Wilder received a PhD in 2014 from the University of California, Riverside. From 2014 to 2015 he was a visiting scholar at Stanford University, focusing on ecological education for indigenous communities. He is co-author of *Plant Life of a Desert Archipelago.*

Andy Wilkinson is a poet, novelist, and songwriter of the Llano Estacado who also teaches creative process in the Honors College of Texas Tech University. Author of *Surprise, Texas,* as well as hundreds of songs and a musical about his relative Charles Goodnight, Wilkinson is most at home in the arid reaches of West Texas. There he has built for Texas Tech Special Collections the largest archive on the history of West Texas musical traditions and for himself a reputation as a singer-storyteller that has led to numerous concerts at the National Cowboy Poetry Festival and elsewhere in the West.

Ofelia Zepeda is Tohono O'odham and professor of linguistics at the University of Arizona in the field of language endangerment and revitalization. As a MacArthur Award–winning poet, she has published several bilingual books and CDs. Her writing and decades as the director of the American Indian Language

Development Institute has been honored with numerous recognitions from her own people and beyond. Her first book of poetry, *Ocean Power: Poems from the Desert*, is considered a classic in Native American literature.

The Southwest Center Series
Joseph C. Wilder, Editor

Bill Broyles and Michael Berman, *Sunshot: Peril and Wonder in the Gran Desierto*

David W. Lazaroff, Philip C. Rosen, and Charles H. Lowe, Jr., *Amphibians, Reptiles, and Their Habitats at Sabino Canyon*

David Yetman, *The Organ Pipe Cactus*

Gloria Fraser Giffords, *Sanctuaries of Earth, Stone, and Light: The Churches of Northern New Spain, 1530–1821*

David Yetman, *The Great Cacti: Ethnobotany and Biogeography*

John Messina, *Álamos, Sonora: Architecture and Urbanism in the Dry Tropics*

Laura L. Cummings, *Pachucas and Pachucos in Tucson: Situated Border Lives*

Bernard L. Fontana and Edward McCain, *A Gift of Angels: The Art of Mission San Xavier del Bac*

David A. Yetman, *The Ópatas: In Search of a Sonoran People*

Julian D. Hayden, *Field Man: The Life of a Desert Archaeologist*, edited by Bill Broyles and Diane Boyer

Bill Broyles, Gayle Harrison Hartmann, Thomas E. Sheridan, Gary Paul Nabhan, and Mary Charlotte Thurtle, *Last Water on the Devil's Highway: A Cultural and Natural History of Tinajas Altas*

Thomas E. Sheridan, *Arizona: A History, Revised Edition*

Richard S. Felger and Benjamin Theodore Wilder, *Plant Life of a Desert Archipelago: Flora of the Sonoran Islands in the Gulf of California*

David Burkhalter, *Baja California Missions: In the Footsteps of the Padres*

Guillermo Núñez Noriega, *Just Between Us: An Ethnography of Male Identity and Intimacy in Rural Communities of Northern Mexico*

Cathy Moser Marlett, *Shells on a Desert Shore: Mollusks in the Seri World*

Rebecca A. Carte, *Capturing the Landscapes of New Spain: Baltasar Obregón and the 1564 Ibarra Expedition*

Gary Paul Nabhan, editor, *Ethnobiology for the Future: Linking Cultural and Ecological Diversity*

James S. Griffith, *Saints, Statues, and Stories: A Folklorist Looks at the Religious Art of Sonora*

David Yetman, Alberto Búrquez, Kevin Hultine, and Michael Sanderson, with Frank S. Crosswhite, *The Saguaro Cactus: A Natural History*

Carolyn Niethammer, *A Desert Feast: Celebrating Tucson's Culinary Heritage*

Gary Paul Nabhan, editor, *The Nature of Desert Nature*